KU-681-515

Rembrandt

2

Rembrandt

DR. SUSANNA PARTSCH

Weidenfeld and Nicolson, London

Author's Note

Most captions to the illustrations include numbers preceded by 'Bredius' which refer to the complete catalogue by A. Bredius, *Rembrandt Paintings (Rembrandt Gemälde)*, Vienna 1935.

Illustration p.2:

Self-portrait, 1632
Wood, 63.5 x 47 cm. Bredius 17
Glasgow, Art Gallery and Museum

First published in Great Britain in 1991 by
George Weidenfeld & Nicolson Limited
91 Clapham High Street, London SW4 7TA

Translated from the German by Terry Bond in association with
First Edition Translations Ltd, Cambridge

Coordination and production: Smeets Illustrated Projects, Weert
Phototypesetting: Royal Smeets Offset b.v., Weert
Print: Royal Smeets Offset b.v., Weert, The Netherlands

ISBN 0 297 83123 2

© Royal Smeets Offset b.v., Weert, The Netherlands

All Rights Reserved. No part of this publication may be reproduced,
stored in a retrieval system, or transmitted, in any form or by any means,
electronic, mechanical, photocopying, recording or otherwise
without the prior permission of the Copyright owner.

Contents

Outline biography   6

I.   Rembrandt and his age   8
    – The war of independence
    – Conflict within the Reformed Church: Calvinists versus
       Remonstrants
    – The 'Golden Age'
    – Art and artists in the Netherlands of the seventeenth
       century
    – The changing face of Rembrandt

II.   Beginnings: childhood, youth and training   22
    – Early work
    – Rembrandt and Lievens – friends and fellow–artists
    – The early self–portraits

III.   Rembrandt's career in Amsterdam   48
    – The early portraits
    – Saskia: wife and model
    – Rembrandt's pictures for the court in The Hague
    – Mythological themes
    – The biblical histories
    – Landscapes
    – The teacher and his studio practice

IV.   The mature years   115
    – *The Night Watch*
    – Saskia's death
    – The biblical histories of the 1640s
    – Portraits and studies of heads

V.   Loss of independence: final works   146
    – Insolvency
    – The later pictures
    – The final commissions
    – The final years
    – The laughing painter

VI.   Research and the problem of attribution   191

Bibliography   196

Index   198

Outline biography

1606	Rembrandt Harmenszoon van Rijn born on 15 July in Leiden. He is the ninth child of the miller Harmen Gerritsz. van Rijn and his wife Cornelia (Neeltje) van Suijtbroek, a baker's daughter.
1613	Rembrandt begins at the Latin School in Leiden. After his brothers take over his father's mill and the bakery belonging to his mother's family, his parents want to give him a better education.
1620	On 20 May Rembrandt matriculates *pro forma* at the Faculty of Philosophy of the University of Leiden.
c. 1621–4	Rembrandt apprenticed to the Leiden painter Jakob van Swanenburgh.
c. 1624	After concluding his apprenticeship Rembrandt goes to Amsterdam in order to complete his studies under the history painter Pieter Lastman.
c. 1625	Rembrandt returns home to Leiden after six months and sets up as a freelance painter. He works closely with Jan Lievens.
1628	Gerrit Dou becomes Rembrandt's first apprentice. In November the stadtholder's secretary, Constantijn Huygens, comes to Leiden and becomes acquainted with Rembrandt's and Jan Lievens' work.
1631	With the help of the art dealer Hendrick Uylenburgh Rembrandt becomes known in Amsterdam. In the autumn of the same year he moves to Amsterdam and works temporarily in Uylenburgh's art dealership.
1632	The stadtholder, Frederik Hendrik, orders several pictures from Rembrandt, among them the five paintings from the Passion series.
1633	On 25 June Rembrandt becomes engaged to Saskia Uylenburgh, the niece of Hendrick Uylenburgh. She is a patrician's daughter from Friesland.
1634	On 2 July Saskia and Rembrandt are married in Friesland. In the same year the painter enters the Guild of St Luke and from then on is entitled to work in Amsterdam as a free-lance painter. He leaves Uylenburgh's art dealership and establishes his own studio.
1635	In December Saskia's and Rembrandt's first son, Rombertus, is born. He dies after two months.
1636	We know from letters to Constantijn Huygens that Rembrandt is living in *Nieuwe Doelenstraat*.
1638	In July the couple's first daughter, Cornelia I, is born. She dies a short time later.
1639	Rembrandt, one of the most respected painters in Amsterdam, buys an imposing house in *Sint Anthonisbreestraat*, demonstrating his climb up the social ladder.
1640	In July the couple's second daughter, Cornelia II, is born. She too lives only a few weeks.

1641	Birth of Rembrandt's son Titus, who is christened on 22 September. Rembrandt is working on *The Night Watch*.
1642	Saskia dies on 14 July. Titus is just 9 months old. Rembrandt engages Geertghe Dircx as a nanny. For the next few years she is his life companion.
1643–9	Rembrandt's work stagnates.
1649	Rembrandt separates from Geertghe Dircx. The 22-year-old Hendrickje Stoffels becomes Rembrandt's new life companion.
1653	The house in *Breestraat* is not paid for except for a very small deposit. The creditors notify Rembrandt that the residual debt is payable. Rembrandt again borrows money and promises to repay it within a year.
1654	The pregnant Hendrickje is summoned to appear in court and accused of being a whore. In October she gives birth to Rembrandt's daughter Cornelia III.
1656	In order to escape his creditors, who are threatening him with debtors' prison, Rembrandt files a petition in honourable insolvency. In July an inventory of his belongings is compiled; it gives details of a large collection of art and curiosities.
1657–8	The auction of Rembrandt's art collection raises much less than expected. Rembrandt must also have the house auctioned in the hope of going some way towards satisfying his creditors.
1660	Rembrandt moves with Hendrickje and Titus to the *Rosengracht*. Titus and Hendrickje establish an art dealership, in which Rembrandt is formally employed. Their contract provides that Rembrandt cannot acquire any capital of his own. In this way he evades his creditors' clutches. Nevertheless, he builds up a new art collection and incurs more debts.
1663	Hendrickje Stoffels dies in July.
1665	Titus comes of age and is paid roughly half of the inheritance to which he is actually entitled.
1668	In February Titus marries Magdalena van Loo, who is related to Saskia's family. In September Titus dies.
1669	Titia, the daughter of Titus and Magdalena, is born in March. Rembrandt dies on 4 October. He is buried on 8 October in the *Westerkerk*.

Self–portrait, 1629
Wood, 15.5 x 12.7 cm. Bredius 2
Munich, Alte Pinakothek

Chapter I

Rembrandt and his age

One of Rembrandt's earliest self-portraits (ill. p. 8) depicts the artist as a young man, his eyes fixed on the person opposite, questioning, searching. Although the young eyes are shadowed, one's gaze is drawn unavoidably to them. Self-confidence is balanced by uncertainty. Not until he reached old age did the painter again portray himself with such honesty.

Rembrandt Harmensz. van Rijn was 23 years old when he painted this self-portrait in 1629. He was already a highly respected painter and lived in Leiden, the town of his birth. Two years later he left for Amsterdam and was very soon also regarded as one of the greatest etchers of his time, his fame extending far beyond the borders of his native land.

During the seventeenth century the Netherlands (Low Countries) were in turmoil, with the Dutch provinces' war of independence from Spanish rule in full swing. But the war, known as the Eighty Years' War, was not merely a war of independence; it was also a religious war, for the theological teachings of Martin Luther (1483-1546) and, more particularly, of John Calvin (1509-1564) had been able to gain a foothold in the Netherlands, and many Catholics had gone over to the Reformed Church. In this climate, and even before the end of the Eighty Years' War, a liberal bourgeoisie had emerged in Amsterdam, making it set to become an economic metropolis in the early capitalist mould.

Although Rembrandt's art is not easily classified according to the artistic movements of the age, the times in which he lived nevertheless formed a foundation for his work and any appreciation of Rembrandt is therefore dependent on a knowledge of the historical background against which he worked and of the artist's status at that time.

The war of independence

On account of the Netherlands' economic and cultural florescence at the beginning of the seventeenth century, and despite the fact that until well into the middle of the century the Dutch provinces were fighting for their independence, this period is generally regarded as the 'Golden Age'.

During the Middle Ages the region which we know today as the Netherlands, Belgium and Luxembourg had been divided up into small territories, and during the fourteenth and fifteenth centuries these territories devolved - as far as the northernmost border - to the duchy of Burgundy. Attempts to subordinate the region to rigid central administration repeatedly failed, and in 1477 Mary of Burgundy (1457-1482) was forced to guarantee the towns' and territories' privileges. In 1506 Burgundy - and with it the Dutch provinces - devolved to Charles V (1500-1558), who was elected emperor in 1519, having ascended the Spanish throne in 1516. He divided the entire Netherlands region, now under Spanish sovereignty, into seventeen provinces. His son Philip

(1527-1598) became king of Spain and ruler of the Netherlands in 1555 and was represented there after 1559 by a regent, his half-sister Margaret of Parma (1522-1586). The individual provinces were controlled by stadtholders appointed by Philip. The stadtholder of Holland, Zeeland and Utrecht was William I, Prince of Orange and Nassau (1533-1584).

During his reign Charles V had made the mistake of encroaching upon the privileges of the towns and territories. As a modern - thinking states-man, he had embarked upon a programme of centralisation within the administration and government. When Philip II proceeded with his father's plans, the move brought embittered resistance from the urban population, which was still organised along medieval lines. Added to the fear of losing their autonomy was irritation at Philip's persecution of heretics. The way in which members of the Reformed Church - mainly Calvinists, but also Lutherans - were persecuted, tortured and murdered by the Inquisition went too far even for the Dutch Catholics. On New Year's Eve in 1564 William of Orange articulated this sense of unease, saying: 'Though personally a Catholic by conviction, I cannot approve when princes have the audacity to wish to control the consciences of their subjects and to deny them their freedom of conscience and religious freedom.'[1]

William's speech made its mark, and the regent loosened the reins. Nevertheless, the Calvinists preached impressively against the govern-ment, and their polemic fell on fertile ground. 1566 saw the beginning of Calvinist iconoclasm in Flanders. The rebellion spread quickly and soon reached the northern provinces, whereupon Philip was forced to send a

The Stoning of St Stephen, 1625
Wood, 89.5 x 123.6 cm
Bredius 531A
Lyon, Musée des Beaux–Arts

An Uninterpreted Tale (Palamedes before Agamemnon), 1626
Wood, 90.1 x 121.3 cm
Bredius 460
Leiden, Stedelijk Museum De Lakenhal (on loan from the Netherlands Office for Fine Arts)

Spanish fighting force to the Netherlands under the supreme command of the Duke of Alba (1507-1582). William of Orange, who in 1566 had fled to his native land, also raised an army and marched on the Netherlands. The two fighting forces met for the first time at the Battle of Heiligerlee on 23 May 1568. The date marks the beginning of the Eighty Years' War, a war which ended only with the Treaty of Westphalia in 1648.

In 1579, once William's plan for uniting the seventeen southern and northern provinces of the Netherlands had failed, the seven northern provinces (Holland, Zeeland, Utrecht, Gelderland, Overijssel, Friesland and Groningen) joined forces to form the Union of Utrecht, and in 1581 they seceded from Spain. Though the stadtholder was deprived of his position as the sovereign's executive authority, the office itself was retained. The court in The Hague thus revolved not around a count, duke or king, but around the so-called stadtholder. In 1584 William was assassinated by one of Philip's agents and was succeeded by his son Maurits (1567-1625), and under the latter's half-brother Frederik Hendrik (1584-1647) the office became hereditary.

Although the republic's war of independence lasted until 1648, it was only in its early stages that it was actually fought out in the disputed region. After a twelve years' truce (1609-1621) armed conflicts took place exclusively in the border regions and off the coast. The affluent provinces were not badly hit. Indeed, the population was largely unaffected, especially as both armies consisted predominantly of foreign mercenaries. However, no sooner had the Reformed Church consolidated its position than arguments broke out within its ranks which led to a split. For a while the new liberalism was threatened by the possibility of civil war.

Conflict within the Reformed Church: Calvinists versus Remonstrants

During the 1570s the Calvinists, who at the beginning of the war of independence had represented at most ten per cent of the population, till then predominantly Catholic, began to drive the Catholics out of civil service posts. By the beginning of the truce of 1609 they held power firmly in their hands. It was at this very moment of consolidation, with no external threat in sight, that the differences which existed between members of the Reformed Church began to take on an aggressive form.

The theologian Jacob Arminius (1560-1609), who represented the liberal wing of the Reformed Church, turned against Calvin's doctrine of predestination, according to which the path of every person was predetermined and could not be altered through individual action or belief. In 1609 a ten-day-long dispute broke out between Arminius and the Calvinist fundamentalist Franciscus Gomarus (1563-1641) over the correctness of this question of faith. The dispute could not be resolved, and when Arminius died shortly afterwards his supporters, the Arminians, handed in to the state of Holland a complaint (or 'remonstrance') drawn up by Johannes Uyttenbogaert (1557-1644). This complaint earned them the name 'Remonstrants'. In 1611 the fundamentalists responded with a 'counter-remonstrance' in which their principal demand was that the state should not interfere in religious affairs. These two petitions provoked a public outbreak of the already smouldering dispute over the relationship between state and Church. It was not long before the entire country was taking part. The 'great pensionary' (raadpensionaris) Johan van Oldenbarnevelt (1547-1619) - who as landsadvocaat to the state of Holland held one of the most important offices in the northern Netherlands and who was, in addition, teacher and mentor to the stadtholder Maurits - spoke out for the Remonstrants. But a twelve years' truce negotiated by him in the Dutch-Spanish war had already led to tension between him and the stadtholder, and Maurits took the opportunity to side with the Counter-Remonstrants. As soon as he could prove unauthorised action on the part of Oldenbarnevelt, the latter was arrested; in 1619 he was executed. This victory for the Counter-Remonstrants unleashed a wave of persecution which was directed at the Remonstrants and lasted until Maurits' death. Not until Frederik Hendrik came to power did the persecution come to an end and the Remonstrant Church was finally legalised in 1630.

From then on, members of the different faiths lived in relatively peaceful co-existence in the republic, and particularly in Amsterdam. The Reformed Church was represented by Calvinists, Remonstrants, Mennonites (Anabaptists) and Lutherans. Catholics were also tolerated, although they were not permitted to build churches and could only hold their services in houses which bore no outward sign of their religious appropriation. Even the Jews, who came to Amsterdam in large numbers from Spain and Portugal, were granted civil rights, something unique in Europe at that time. This liberal approach is explained by the region's flourishing trade, which had been assuming an early capitalist character

Tobit Praying for Death, 1626
Wood, 40.1 x 29.9 cm. Bredius 486
Amsterdam, Rijksmuseum

since the turn of the century. The merchants were the most powerful men in the state, and business took priority over the question of faith. There is, in fact, no other explanation for the acceptance of the Jews, who maintained trading links throughout Europe and were thus able to contribute considerably to the growth of the Dutch provinces.

The 'Golden Age'

Traditionally, agriculture and fishing were of great importance to the Dutch. They exported meat, butter and cheese, and also fish, and in return bought grain and other foodstuffs. The herring catch had long been of particular significance. Now larger boats were built in order that the fishermen could travel to Iceland for the cod fishing. In 1612 they also began whale fishing and their summer camps on Spitsbergen were so successful that it was fifty years before their monopoly could be broken.

   The ships used for fishing and fish exporting were only needed during the short summer season. For the rest of the year they were used to transport other goods to the rest of Europe. It was on board these ships that the Dutch discovered a new maritime route to the East Indian spice-growing islands, a route which considerably increased trading opportunities.

The Baptism of the Eunuch, 1626
Wood, 63.5 x 48 cm
Not in Bredius
Utrecht, Rijksmuseum
Het Catharijneconvent

So as not to endanger the enterprise through too much internal competition, the Dutch East Indies Company was founded in 1602 and had the sole right to exploit the islands. This joint-stock company was one of the first to sell shares on the open market, and these were much sought after, Rembrandt being one of its shareholders.

The path which the Netherlands trod to become one of the world's first capitalist states was, however, somewhat strange. Well into the seventeenth century Dutch towns were governed according to medieval laws, and it was not only the threat to their religious freedom but also the threat to these medieval structures which incited the towns to rebellion. It was, to all intents and purposes, a conservative revolt against modern forms of state organisation. Until then, the mercantile system had failed to gain a foothold in the Netherlands. Now, however, the once poor northern provinces began to profit from the fact that the rich southern regions remained under Spanish rule and were disadvantaged by various restrictions. Antwerp was under blockade and could not be considered a large trading centre. Many merchants salvaged their fortunes by transferring them to Amsterdam. Reformed Christians too flocked across the border. The textile industry, until then firmly in the grip of Flanders, also began to flourish in the north. Delft, Haarlem and Leiden found great prosperity. But Amsterdam outstripped them all. In 1550 the town had only 30,000 inhabitants, but by 1630 the number had increased to around 115,000. Unlike Antwerp, Amsterdam had its own merchant fleet and was therefore not reliant on assistance from out of town, and the large trading organisations attracted merchants from every corner of Europe. Amsterdam had also begun to oust Antwerp from her leading position in the money-market. 1609 saw the founding of the city's first bank and 1612 the opening of the stock exchange, both of which opened the door to speculation.

Large-scale economic growth also led to changes in the way of life. The merchants built themselves magnificent houses on the canals, decoration became the order of the day and people pursued a lifestyle appropriate to their standing. Of necessity, these trends also altered the role of art and, as a direct result, the social standing of the artist, which was still determined by a medieval system based on guilds.

Art and artists in the Netherlands in the seventeenth century

Despite the economic upheaval taking place in the Dutch republic in the early seventeenth century, the various professions continued to be organised in guilds, as had been usual since the Middle Ages. Before he was permitted to head a studio of his own, a painter had to join the Guild of St Luke. No distinction was made between painters of the artistic variety and house painters. The notion of the scientifically trained artist with high social standing, as seen in Italy since the Renaissance, was only to be found in Catholic Flanders. (Peter Paul Rubens (1577-1640), who on occasions even served as a diplomat, is the best-known example.) The price of pictures was determined by their size. In general, it was not possible for painters to become wealthy from painting alone, and many were forced to earn a living by working outside the vocation. Most artists came from the middle classes, and only a few succeeded in climbing the social ladder. Rembrandt was one of the few exceptions, albeit only for a short while. Trapped in a social order which ruled out any humanist general

education, the Dutch painters of the seventeenth century could only base their work on a few contemporary artistic theories. In the foreword to his 1604 publication *Het schilderboek (Lives of Painters)*, the best-known theoretician of the day, Karel van Mander (1558-1606) described painting as 'noble and free' and criticised the fact that painters were forced to join craftsmen's guilds. His protests met with no success. Samuel van Hoogstraeten (1627-1678) took up many of van Mander's ideas in his 1678 publication *Einleyding tot de Hooge Schoole der Schilderkonst (Introduction to the High School of Painting, or: The Visible World)*. His writings are a major source of information about Rembrandt, since he had been a pupil of his and shared many of his views.

Hoogstraeten, as well as other theoreticians of the day, classified paintings according to theme. Historical paintings, which included representations of classical, mythological, historical and also biblical events, had the greatest value. Next came scenes in genre style and landscapes, and in last place ranked the still life painting so popular today. Portrait painting was placed both in the first and last categories. On the one hand it was regarded as a form of deception in that it could only give a semblance of reality; on the other hand it was a form of painting in which man took centre stage.

Artists were advised to restrict themselves to the themes of which they had the best command. For the first time in the history of painting artists began to specialise by genre. The choice of theme remained the painter's, as did the style of its depiction. The artist's major goal was *inventio*, inventiveness. The aim was not, however, to prove one's own originality, but to accelerate the progress of art: 'Endeavour with all your strength, oh eager young painters, to train yourselves that you may make your own discoveries. ... Who knows, whether art can become more perfect?'[2]

There was one rule which applied to historical painting in general. According to this, an artist planning a picture had first to study the historical sources so that he might consciously select a moment to depict. Borrowing a good composition was not regarded as a sin, but the painter had to do his utmost to choose a different theme. Even the copying of details from other pictures was legitimate. After studying the sources, it was important that the artist made a sketch to mark out the principal features of the composition. The central figure had to be accentuated in such a way as to ensure that the beholder's first glance fell upon him and not upon the secondary figures.

There were, then, certain guidelines within which the artist was expected to work. On the other hand, the free market which had emerged as a result of recent economic changes obeyed its own laws, and these often contradicted those of the theoreticians. In the art market, landscapes, scenes in genre style and still life paintings were, for example, in great demand, whereas historical scenes were much less sought after. Only very occasionally did the artist work for a customer, but if he was working on a commission exactly which moment he should select or precisely how the composition should look was no longer stipulated, with the result that he was afforded greater freedom than traditional artistic guidelines permitted, but was also expected to demonstrate greater knowledge.

The commissions most sought after were those which came from the stadtholder's court in The Hague, for the artist could often expect to be

16

Child with Dead Peacocks, c. 1639
Canvas, 145 x 135.5 cm
Bredius 456
Amsterdam, Rijksmuseum

paid fifty to one hundred times the usual price for a painting. However, the opportunities were limited to only a few privileged artists and for the most part to just a few works. One of these privileged artists was Rembrandt, who in fact received a relatively large number of official commissions. In addition to the stadtholder's court and attendant nobility, the government, regents and guilds also played a major part as wealthy customers. As a result of the Reformation, which forbade religious imagery in its churches, however, the Church, which in Catholic regions was still a major source of employment, had lost almost all significance as a customer in the Dutch republic.

Instead, the Dutch artists' major customer was the bourgeoisie. Well-to-do middle-class citizens ordered portraits and bought pictures on the open market to decorate their houses. But the desire for decoration was not exclusively the domain of the rich middle-class citizen in the town; even craftsmen and farmers frequently earned so well amidst the general prosperity that they could afford to buy paintings. Thus the economic upturn, and also the social changes which had taken place as a result of the Reformation, played an important part in the development of Dutch painting in the seventeenth century. The value of these factors in assessing an artist is often overlooked by researchers.

The changing face of Rembrandt

Over the years, Rembrandt has been viewed in many different lights and his work interpreted in a variety of ways. In the nineteenth century, for example, he was seen as an uneducated miller's son, an unappreciated

Self–portrait
with a Dead Bittern, 1639
Wood, 121 x 89 cm. Bredius 31
Dresden, Staatliche
Kunstsammlungen,
Gemäldegalerie

17

Bathsheba being Groomed for King David, c. 1633
Wood, 110.5 x 94.3 cm
Bredius 494
Ottawa, National Gallery
of Canada

genius who died in poverty. The outsider for which he had been taken in the eighteenth century became, in the eyes of his fellow-countrymen, a revolutionary who had fought for the bourgeoisie and the Protestant faith. A national hero, his statue was erected in Amsterdam in 1852. In the twentieth century the emphasis has largely shifted to his work, particularly his chiaroscuro paintings, and the fragmentary details of his biography have not been allowed too great an influence. He has been acclaimed a genius, a man who worked without models and created Bible illustrations from his imagination alone, using only the relevant text from the Bible as a basis for his work. The legend of the poor miller's son who had received no humanist education persisted for a long time. It is a legend created by Rembrandt's early biographers. For example, in his *Teutschen Academie der edlen Bau-, Bild-, und Mahlerey-Künste (German Academy of the Noble Arts of Architecture, Sculpture and Painting),* published in Nuremberg in 1675, Joachim von Sandrart (1606-1688), a contemporary of Rembrandt, wrote: 'It is a remarkable thing that the admirable Rembrandt, springing as he did from a flat marshy country, and having the background of a miller, should yet have been so driven by nature towards the noblest art that he reached a surprising height of achievement both by his natural bent and by his application.'[3]

The Holy Family, c. 1634
Canvas, 183.5 x 123 cm.
Bredius 544
Munich, Alte Pinakothek

Sandrart was not the only early biographer of Rembrandt; Filippo Baldinucci (1624-1696) dedicated a chapter to him in his 1686 volume of artists' biographies. The most detailed portrayal of Rembrandt is to be found, however, in a treatise entitled *De Groote Schouburgh de*

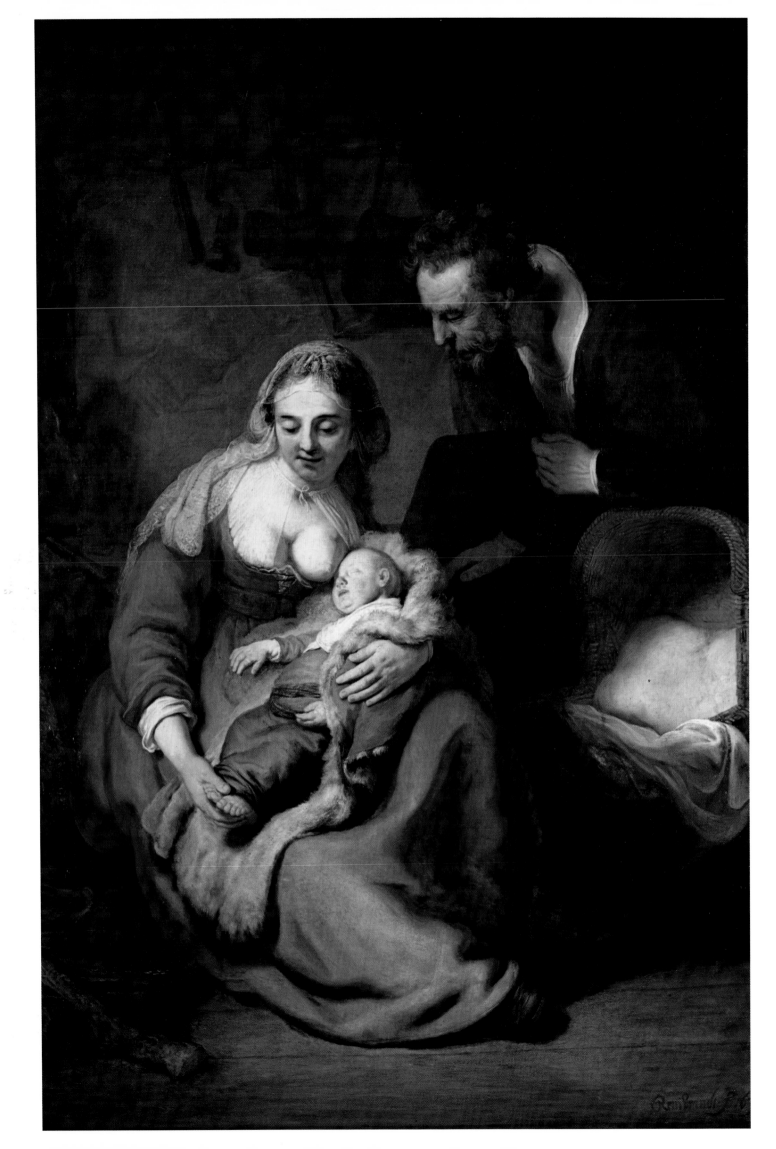

*Hannah and Simeon
in the Temple*, *c.* 1627–1628
Wood, 55.4 x 43.7 cm. Bredius 535
Hamburg, Kunsthalle

Nederlantsche Konstschilders (The Great Theatre of Dutch Artists), published by Arnold Houbraken (1660-1719) in 1718. Although we now know from information which has since come to light that these early biographers were mistaken about many of the details of Rembrandt's life, they have been and are still quoted time and time again.

The changing face of Rembrandt over the centuries is reflected in the wealth of literature which has been published about him, for every age has tried - from a different standpoint - to interpret the painter and his work. For a long time, for instance, researchers have battled against the highly stylised picture of Rembrandt conjured up by Julius Langbehn (1851-1907) in his 1890 book *Rembrandt als Erzieher (Rembrandt as an Educator)*, in which the painter is portrayed as an educator of the German people, his truly northern art reflecting both inner warmth and national spirit. It was in Langbehn's writings that terms such as 'racial purity', 'sound patriotism' and 'degeneration' first appeared. He did not seriously study the artist and his work, yet by propagating this imaginary picture of Rembrandt he was promulgating ideas which would later be seized upon by the Nazis.

It has not been easy to repair the damage done by these totally unscientific and for the most part downright fabricated representations of Rembrandt, for despite the publication since the beginning of this century of many serious biographies, such false interpretations have been dogged in their persistence. Today research has entered a new phase. Following the compilation by Abraham Bredius and Otto Benesch of huge catalogues of Rembrandt's work, we are now seeing the publication of extensive volumes of research carried out by the Rembrandt Research Project, which has tested every picture attributed to Rembrandt for authenticity. The artist's work has shrunk. In 1923 744 paintings were still thought to be authentic, but since then the number has been falling steadily. In 1935 Bredius published a catalogue of Rembrandt's paintings which contained only 639 works. The revised edition published by Horst Gerson in 1969 listed only 420 paintings as authentic, and since then the number has fallen further.

In addition to these questions of attribution (which are dealt with in detail on pages 190 to 195), there are also other difficulties. In recent years, for example, the question of Rembrandt's genius has been brought into question. Christian Tümpel, for instance, contradicts many biographers and claims to have proof that the painter lacked innovation in his choice of themes and composition and preferred to use models. Gary Schwartz sees in him a supporter of the Remonstrants and translator of their ideas into pictures. Moreover, Schwartz suggests that despite many attempts Rembrandt did not succeed in gaining admission to patrician cliques and thus becoming a successful painter. Both researchers have uncovered many new and significant facts which undoubtedly cast the artist in a more objective light, yet in their striving to put an end once and for all to the Rembrandt legend they have drawn a very limited picture of the painter. Quite the opposite effect is achieved, however, by the research of Svetlana Alpers, who, although she draws on both works, does not, in doing so, lose sight of Rembrandt the artist.

Although the body of literature about Rembrandt has now become so unwieldy that it is no longer possible to obtain an overview, there are many questions which have still to be answered properly. Often this shortcoming is disguised by plausible-sounding guesswork which for a while appears to have some validity but is then replaced by other guesswork. Despite the work of the large-scale Rembrandt Research Project in the Netherlands, the final judgement on this painter is not likely to be made for some time.

1   Cit. in Haak 1984, p. 17

2   S. Hoogstraeten, cit. in Haak 1984, p. 65

3   Cit. in L. Goldscheider, *Rembrandt. Gemälde und Graphik (Rembrandt. Paintings and sketches)*, London 1960, p. 11 (also in T. Copplestone, *Rembrandt*, London 1960, p. 69)

Chapter II

Beginnings: childhood, youth and training

Rembrandt Harmensz. van Rijn was born on 15 July 1606 in Leiden. His father, Harmen Gerritsz. (c.1568-1640) came from an old-established and respected family of millers. As the joint owner of a mill, he belonged to the moneyed middle classes. The location of the mill on the Old Rhine enabled him to append the surname van Rijn ('on the Rhine') to his own, and this became his children's family name. In 1589 he married Cornelia (Neeltje) van Suijtbroeck (c.1568-1640), a baker's daughter from an old patrician family. Both had converted to Calvinism before their marriage.

At the time, the processing of grain was a lucrative business, and the Dutch knew how to exploit the bad conditions of domestic trade. When the harvest was good they bought up grain from all over Europe, stored

Jakob Isaaksz. van Swanenburgh (1571-1638)
The Sibyl Showing Aeneas the Underworld, Date unknown
Wood, 93.5 x 124 cm
Leiden, Stedelijk Museum De Lakenhal

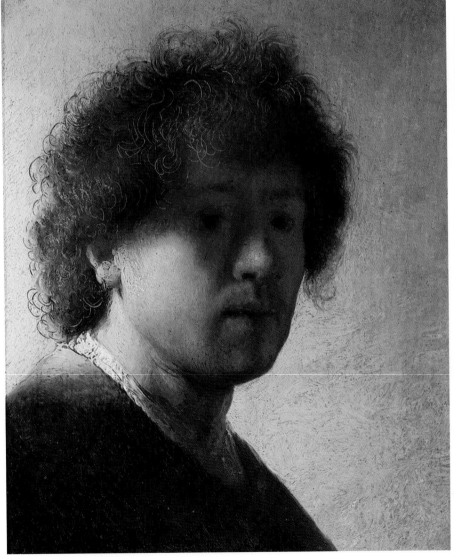

Self–portrait, c. 1628
Wood, 22.5 x 18.6 cm
Not in Bredius
Amsterdam, Rijksmuseum

it in their corn-lofts and sold it at a huge profit in times of famine. When Rembrandt was born the van Rijns already had four sons to carry on the family tradition. Rembrandt also had a younger sister. Four other children had died at an early age. From the *Beschrijvinge der Stadt Leyden (Description of the City of Leiden)* published by the burgomaster Jan Orlers (1570-1646) in 1614 and revised in 1641, we know an astonishing amount about the education and training of the young Rembrandt. Although a few inconsistencies repeatedly provoke researchers to produce new hypotheses, it is safe to assume that the young Rembrandt was sent by his parents to the Latin School at the age of 7 or 9. They wished to enable their son to study subsequently at the noted University of Leiden, founded in 1575, and in 1620 he did indeed matriculate. However, it is unclear whether he actually took up his studies or merely wished to make use of the privileges which he was entitled to claim as a student. According to Orlers, Rembrandt 'hadn't the least urge or inclination in that direction, his natural bent being for painting and drawing only.'[4] His parents yielded and in 1619 or 1620 sent him as an apprentice to the then respected Leiden painter Jakob Isaaksz. van Swanenburgh (1571-1638). The Catholic Swanenburgh was known chiefly for his vivid depictions of hell and witchcraft, which had brought him into conflict with the Inquisition several times during his long sojourn in Naples. Rembrandt learned from his first teacher how to translate human reactions such as

Rembrandt's Mother (?), c. 1630
Wood, 61 x 47.4 cm. Bredius 70
Windsor Castle, Royal Collection

The Prophet Balaam and the Ass,
1626
Wood, 65 x 47 cm. Bredius 487
Paris, Musée Cognacq–Jay

grief, desperation and joy convincingly into the language of pictures; how to use darkness and light meaningfully in order to separate the important from the unimportant; and also how to limit himself to relatively small formats.

At the end of the apprenticeship, Rembrandt's father sent his son to the then famous history painter Pieter Lastman (1583-1633) in Amsterdam to complete his studies. Lastman had returned to Amsterdam in 1607 after a lengthy period of study in Italy and was now gathering around him a group of established painters. The majority of them lived in *Sint Anthonisbreestraat*, where Rembrandt would also later reside. Now, during his first period in Amsterdam, he made a great number of contacts, but more importantly learned from his teacher. According to Orlers, Rembrandt returned to Leiden six months later in order to 'paint for himself alone'. He was 17 years old.

Early work

When Rembrandt returned to Leiden he had already completed his training as a painter. Now he worked in his own studio and had pupils of his own. Whether he was 16 or 20 years old at this time - that is, whether he finished his apprenticeship in 1622 or not until 1626 - is the subject of debate among researchers even today. The fact that his earliest dated picture, *The Stoning of St Stephen* (ill. p. 9) is dated 1625 would militate in favour of a later date, perhaps around 1625/26. There is also no evidence from any source to suggest that he kept a studio jointly with his fellow-painter Jan Lievens (1607-1674), as has long been assumed. All that can be shown is that the two painters worked closely together and profited from mutual stimulation. By 1628 at the latest Rembrandt was taking on apprentices at his studio. The first of his pupils whom we know by name was Gerard Dou (1613-1675).

Pieter Lastman (1583–1633)
*Balaam's Ass Balking
before the Angel,* 1622
Wood, 41.3 x 60.3 cm.
New York, private collection

*Christ Driving the Money–
changers out of the Temple,* 1626
Wood, 43.1 x 32 cm. Bredius 532
Moscow, Pushkin Museum

Self–portrait, 1629
Wood, 89.5 x 73.5 cm. Bredius 8
Boston, Isabelle Stewart Gardner
Museum

*David Playing the
Harp before Saul*, *c.* 1629
Wood, 61.8 x 50.2 cm. Bredius 490
Frankfurt, Städelsches
Kunstinstitut

Unlike the majority of his fellow-painters, Rembrandt did not restrict himself to one theme. In addition to the historical paintings for which he was predestined after his training under Lastman, he also worked on studies of heads, portraits and self-portraits during this first Leiden period.

In the beginning he still adhered very closely in his historical paintings to the tradition passed on to him by Lastman. This can be seen clearly from the two paintings *The Stoning of St Stephen* of 1625 and *An Uninterpreted Tale* (ill. p. 10), which he painted a year later. At the time he preferred strong, almost garish colours, well-peopled scenes and a wealth of detail. The stories which he attempted to depict still captivated him to such an extent that he lost himself in them. In the *St Stephen* the central figure, the kneeling martyr, is positioned in the lower part of the frame. At the centre stands one of the three stone-throwing assassins. Both the architectonic landscape in the background and the presence of several people who are immaterial to the story leave the beholder with a sense of *horror vacui*. In his most recent publication Gary Schwartz has linked these two early paintings with the humanist Petrus Scriverius. Drawing on various family and neighbourhood links, he construes an acquaintance between Scriverius and Rembrandt and surmises that the two paintings were commissioned by the former. Basing his ideas on

The Money–changer, 1627
Wood, 31.9 x 42.5 cm. Bredius 420
Berlin–Dahlem, Staatliche Museen,
Gemäldegalerie

Christ at Emmaus, c. 1628–1629
Paper on wood, 37.4 x 42.3 cm
Bredius 539
Paris, Musée Jacquemart–André

other research, he interprets the so far uninterpreted tale as *Palamedes before Agamemnon*. He establishes a link with the unjust death sentence passed upon Johan van Oldenbarnevelt (cf. p. 11) and interprets the work as support for the Remonstrants inspired by Scriverius. Palamedes was a character from the Trojan Wars who, having seen through the cunning with which Odysseus hoped to avoid the war, exposed him. Forced in this way to go along to Troy, Odysseus plotted his revenge. He concealed a fake conspiratorial letter from Priam, the ruler of Troy, threw in some gold coins and saw to it that the package was discovered, where-upon Palamedes was stoned to death. A 1625 stage play on this theme alluded to the murder of Oldenbarnevelt. At first glance Schwartz's theories are tempting. However, they are based on a great many assumptions for which there is no evidence in the pictures. Furthermore, Rembrandt's relationship with Scriverius and other citizens of Leiden cannot be assured despite Schwartz's study of historical sources.

Rembrandt did not adhere to the style of his early historical pictures for long. Under the influence of the Utrecht painters, who took an intense interest in the works of Caravaggio (1573-1610), he discovered a completely new style, which led him to concentrate primarily on small

Hendrick Goudt (1582/83–1610)
*Jupiter and Mercury in the House
of Philemon and Baucis*,
Engraving from 1612 after a
painting from 1608–1609
16.4 x 22 cm
Amsterdam, Rijksmuseum

scenes. This new style was visible as early as 1627 in a painting from that year which until recently was interpreted as a scene in the genre style and had acquired the title *The Money-changer* (ill. p. 28). Tümpel has now demonstrated that it is, in fact, a biblical story, an illustration of the parable directed against avarice from Chapter 12 of the Gospel according to St Luke. The story is that of a farmer whose harvest is so rich that there is not room for it in his barn. The farmer plans to build a new barn in which to stock-pile his fortune and keep it all for himself, but then the Lord speaks to him, saying 'Thou fool, this night thy soul shall be required of thee: then whose shall those things be, which thou hast provided? So is he that layeth up treasure for himself, and is not rich toward God.'[5]

Hans Holbein the Younger (1497-1543) had established a tradition of painting this parable which other painters had borrowed. The resulting depictions were adorned with many details, such as Death and the partly built barn. Rembrandt, on the other hand, concentrated on the corn farmer. In a room with furnishings and walls disappearing into the darkness, an old man sits at a table surrounded by books, papers, bags of

Peter and Paul
in Conversation, c. 1628
Wood, 72.3 x 59.5 cm. Bredius 423
Melbourne, National Gallery of
Victoria

money and gold ducats. In his left hand he holds a candle and in the gleam of light from it he is looking at a coin. With the hand in which he holds the coin, he is also carefully shading the flame as if to keep it from blowing out. Both this and the books hint at transience. The Hebrew characters on the papers indicate that this is a scene from the Bible.

By comparing this with the two pictures described previously it is possible to recognise the development which had taken place in Rembrandt's work in the short space of time between 1625 and 1627. Apart from the fact that he concentrated scrupulously on a particular moment in the action, as his pupil Hoogstraeten later demanded in his own theory of art, Rembrandt now favoured indoor scenes. He found his models for these primarily in Bible illustrations and in the graphic arts. Painters had generally preferred landscapes as a background in historical pictures. However, in the chiaroscuro style of painting favoured by Caravaggio and the Utrecht painters Rembrandt found a style with which he could single out the important elements of the painting. This type of composition was better suited to indoor representations, and so Rembrandt went in search, apparently deliberately, of themes which could, or even had to, take place in rooms. As time passed he inevitably not only developed new methods of depiction, but also found subjects - albeit subjects which did not belong to any painting tradition - which were suited to his painting technique.

Paul in Prison, 1627
Wood, 72.8 x 60.2 cm. Bredius 601
Stuttgart, Staatsgalerie

This said, the next example is an exception. *Christ at Emmaus* (ill. p. 29) had been depicted often since the Middle Ages, but never before had the scene been represented in pictures in the way chosen by the young Rembrandt in 1628. In Chapter 24 of the Gospel according to St Luke the story is told of two disciples who go to Emmaus on the day of the Resurrection. They meet the risen Christ, but do not recognise him and tell him what has happened in Jerusalem. In the evening they invite him to stay with them in Emmaus. 'And it came to pass, as he sat at meat with them, he took bread, and blessed it, and brake, and gave to them. And their eyes were opened, and they knew him.'

Rembrandt selects the moment in which the disciples recognise Christ and illustrates it simply through his use of light which illuminates the terrified faces. One disciple sitting opposite Christ is bathed in light. He is raising his hands in terror and recoiling. The second is already kneeling at the feet of the risen Christ. In the shaded regions of the painting he is barely perceptible. From the point of view of the beholder, Christ himself is lit from behind. His body is shadowed; only its outline stands out. This scene is pushed into the right-hand side of the picture. On the left, in the background, the innkeeper's wife is illuminated gently by a fire in the stove. Its light barely penetrates the parlour of the inn, and she does not observe the incident. By the beginning of this century it was already recognised that Rembrandt had used as his model for the composition of this picture an engraving from 1612 which had been cut by Hendrick Goudt (1582/83-1648) after a painting by Adam Elsheimer (1578-1610), the theme of which was *Jupiter and Mercury in the House of Philemon and Baucis*. Here too the gods are illuminated by a source of light which cannot be clearly identified.

Christ at Emmaus also illustrates one of Rembrandt's working methods and one which Hoogstraeten later expressly permits in his 1678 *Inleyding tot de Hooge Schoole der Schilderkonst (Introduction to the High School of Painting)*: 'None the less and notwithstanding, you will be permitted, if you find from time to time a well-ordered piece, to borrow the manner of its depiction, i.e. its method of communication and the manner of its arrangement ... But you should strive to use a different material ...'[6] It was thus entirely legitimate for an artist to make use of a model, but essential that he chose a different theme for its translation. Whether Rembrandt was so moved by the engraving that he searched for a suitable theme into which to translate it on canvas and found this in the Emmaus episode, or whether he had already decided on the subject and went in search of a suitable model, is a matter for debate. What is certain is that in his early period he did search for possible indoor scenes, since these enabled him to use the chiaroscuro technique to its best effect.

In the same year as the disciples in Emmaus were painted, Rembrandt painted a picture which for a long time baffled researchers (ill. p. 30). Suggested themes included *Two Scholars Disputing, Hippocrates and Democritus* and even *Two Seated Apostles*, and all were food for thought for the art historians. Now Christian Tümpel has come up with a new interpretation. He is of the opinion that the picture is of the apostles Peter and Paul, who are meeting for the first time and discussing the gospel. This suggestion is supported by the fact that Paul is traditionally depicted with a long face and a beard, as is the figure who is shown head-on and pointing to a place in the opened book which is resting on the knees of the figure with his back to the beholder. Although this figure's face is turned towards Paul and is thus not visible, the round head, whiskers and garland of curls enable us to deduce the identity of the figure, since all are symbols which have characterised Peter since the earliest depictions. The light falls on the two arguing men and on the book, which represents both their scholarliness and the Scriptures. Other symbols, such as the globe, which alludes to the apostles' missionary work worldwide, and the extinguished candle, a symbol for the Old Testament, lie in the shadows. The symbols typically used to represent the two apostles, the key and the sword, have been left out. The theory that these two men are Peter and Paul is corroborated by another picture, *Paul in Prison* (ill. p. 31), which Rembrandt had painted earlier, in 1627. In this picture the old man illuminated by the light falling through the prison bars is clearly identifiable as Paul on account of his sword, which is leaning against the bed. Though the features have been modified slightly in the Peter and Paul painting, they are nevertheless of the same type: a long face with a beard, a high, furrowed brow and combed-back hair. In this picture of Paul, one of Rembrandt's earliest indoor depictions, the artist succeeds in emphasising not only the theme of *Paul in Prison*, which acquired its tradition as a result of Paul's frequent imprisonment during the apostles' missionary work, but also his scientific character, which was reflected both in his letters and in his interpretation of the gospel.

Even during his Leiden period Rembrandt became so familiar with

Jeremiah Lamenting the Destruction of Jerusalem (?), 1630 Wood, 58.3 x 46.6 cm. Bredius 604 Amsterdam, Rijksmuseum

Andromeda, c. 1630
Wood, 34.5 x 25 cm. Bredius 462
The Hague, Mauritshuis

Anonymous artist from the
mid–ninth century
Andromeda, after a leaf from
a lost ancient *codex of the Aratea,*
Parchment, 22.5 x 20 cm.
Leiden, Bibliotheek der
Rijksuniversiteit

chiaroscuro techniques that he was able to abandon the indoor setting as
an artistic vehicle in favour of natural light out-of-doors. This is shown
in a superb painting from 1630, which, as a result of it still not having
been interpreted with any certainty, has acquired the provisional title
Jeremiah Lamenting the Destruction of Jerusalem (ill. p. 33). In the foreground, an old man leans on a huge truncated column. His head rests in
his hand, his arm on the Bible. His bare foot lies on a splendid carpet,
and next to him stands a lavishly decorated bowl filled with all manner of
valuable objects. A wide, brightly lit strip separates him from a burning
town which is being captured by soldiers and from which people are
fleeing. The fire glimmers only dimly in contrast to the bright light in
which the protagonist is bathed.

From this picture it is clear that Rembrandt, through his reduction of
everything to the essentials, his omission of characteristic symbols and
also often his redesigns of previously painted pictures, makes it difficult
for the viewer to identify his depictions. The symbols of which he does
make use are frequently difficult to interpret, and it has often required
detailed research before a theme could be labelled with any certainty.

This is the reason for the dogged persistence of the legend of the artist
whose themes were conjured up by his own imagination. It was easy to
visualise Rembrandt as a child listening as the grown-ups read the Bible
aloud to each other and resolving even then to paint it all some day.
Moreover, as a Protestant artist, he was said to have rejected the Catholic

An Old Woman Reading:
Rembrandt's Mother as the
Prophetess Hannah, 1631
Wood, 59.8 x 47.7 cm. Bredius 69
Amsterdam, Rijksmuseum

artistic tradition and to use only texts from the Bible as the basis of his work. From a historical point of view, this is certainly untrue. Although in the seventeenth century the supporters of the various religious groups argued about liturgical matters and questions of dogma and ecclesiastical history, the painters of the day nevertheless referred to the traditional sources of the Bible, legends handed down from father to son and also the Jewish military leader and historiographer Flavius Josephus' work *The Antiquities of the Jews.* Although a Calvinist, Rembrandt had learned his craft from two Catholic painters, and his paintings were bought by people of all faiths. Neither would have been possible had there been a dogmatic division between 'Catholic' and 'Protestant' painting. The methods characteristic of Rembrandt's work can be seen not only in his biblical paintings, but also in his few works on mythological themes. In 1629 or 1630 he painted the picture *Andromeda* (ill. p. 34). According to mythology, Andromeda's mother, Cassiopeia, had provoked the wrath of the gods by claiming to be more beautiful than all of the Nereids (goddesses of the sea). The resulting plagues, floods and monster which visited the land could only be banished through the sacrifice of Andromeda. Chained to a rock, Andromeda hoped for a hero who would rescue her from the menacing monster. And the hero did indeed materialise, in the shape of Perseus.

Simeon in the Temple, 1631
Wood, 60.9 x 47.8 cm. Bredius 543
The Hague, Mauritshuis

36

Judas Returning the Thirty Pieces of Silver, 1629
Wood, 79 x 102.3 cm
Bredius–Gerson 539A
England, private collection

Normally, of course, Andromeda was depicted with the monster and the approaching Perseus. Rembrandt, however, concentrated exclusively on the princess, whom he depicted half-naked and chained to a rock. Only the light which falls across her body contains the promise of rescue; thus she is turning her head expectantly towards it. Rembrandt found the model for his Andromeda in a medieval manuscript in which the motif had been borrowed from an astronomical textbook from the ancient world. This ninth-century codex is to be found in Leiden. Moreover, the motif had been distributed since 1609 in the form of a copperplate engraving. It can be seen then, even from his early work, that Rembrandt's method when choosing a theme was first to make a study of historical sources and to search for suitable models. Then he selected a particular moment which he depicted economically, dispensing with any detail which he felt to be unnecessary. For him, man was the focus. Gestures and facial expressions as well as the light - to which symbolic meaning was often attached - frequently had to suffice as an explanation of the scene. This form of historical painting was developed during

Rembrandt's Leiden period, when he worked closely with the painter Jan Lievens. The stimulation and encouragement which they drew from each other is of considerable importance.

Rembrandt and Lievens - friends and fellow-artists

For a long time researchers were agreed that Jan Lievens (1607-1674) and Rembrandt had shared a studio in Leiden. Moreover, there was no reason to doubt the suggestion that the one-year-younger Lievens had always stood in Rembrandt's shadow. Today we are having to revise these views. In his 1641 *Description of the City of Leiden*, Jan Orlers gives a detailed account of Jan Lievens' career. He did not, as Rembrandt did, attend the Latin School, but was apprenticed at the age of 8 to a painter. Two years later his father sent him to Lastman in Amsterdam. At the age of 12 he returned home and henceforth worked as a freelance artist. Stylistically, his time with Lastman had made very little impression on him. Instead, he turned to the Utrecht Caravaggists and the Haarlem Classicists, then the most modern schools of Dutch painting. By the time Rembrandt returned to Leiden from Amsterdam Lievens was already an established painter there.

Jan Orlers gave a much more detailed account of Lievens than of Rembrandt. He described individual pictures and named the owners of paintings. In short, he saw Lievens as the more important painter. He did not, however, make mention of a shared studio. Whether or not it existed will have to remain speculation. What is certain is that the two painters soon entered upon a lively exchange. For the most part, Rembrandt painted small-format historical pictures, Lievens large-format half-lengths. Yet Rembrandt profited from the influence which the Caravaggists had had on Lievens. It was as a result of the ideas to which he was exposed through Lievens that he began to develop his particular form of chiaroscuro. In those first years in Leiden Rembrandt obviously felt challenged by Lievens' painting, but by 1628 the tables appear to have turned. Svetlana Alpers describes the relationship between the two painters as an early - for the Dutch art world of the day, unique - example of a friendship between artists, a friendship comparable to that between Georges Braques (1882-1963) and Pablo Picasso (1881-1973). 'And here too, it was the artist who in the course of time proved the weaker who was first the leader.'[7]

These roles were also ascribed to the two young artists by Constantijn Huygens, the son of Christiaen Huygens (1551-1624), secretary to both the stadtholder and the Council of State. Although Huygens senior gave his sons, who later shared this office, a humanist education, he did not permit Constantijn to follow his inclinations and become a painter. As secretary to the art-loving stadtholder Frederik Hendrik, Constantijn at least had the opportunity later to take an interest in painting as a connoisseur and collector. In 1628, in his capacity as secretary to the stadtholder, Constantijn Huygens came to Leiden and there he visited the by then well-known painters Lievens and Rembrandt. The visit had far-reaching consequences for the young painters, partly in that it enabled them to win commissions from the court in The Hague. In his autobiography, a priceless source of information written shortly afterwards but not discovered until 1897, Huygens gives his impressions of this visit.[8] He commends the great talent of both painters:

Jan Lievens (1607–1674)
Constantijn Huygens
(1596–1687), c. 1628
Wood, 99 x 84 cm.
Amsterdam, Rijksmuseum
(on loan from the Musée de la Chartreuse, Douai)

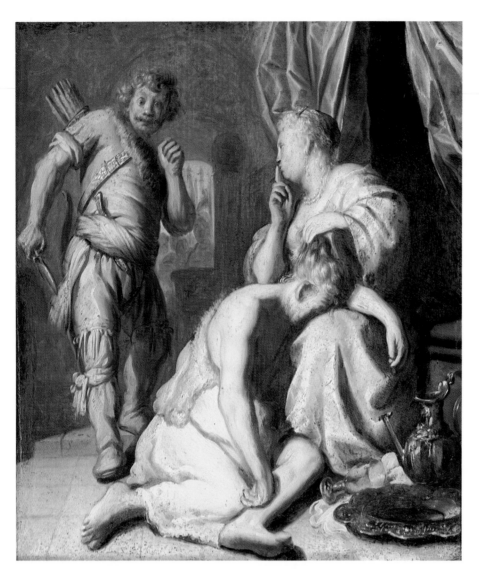

Jan Lievens (1607–1674)
The Capture of Samson, 1627–1628
Wood, 27.5 x 23.5 cm
Amsterdam, Rijksmuseum

'the youngsters owe nothing to their teachers, and all to their own gifts. In fact, I am actually convinced that even if no one had set them an example, even if they had been left on their own all their lives and developed a strong inclination towards painting, they would have reached the same heights they have now attained - under guidance, as people erroneously believe.'

But Huygens also voiced criticism, pointing out their 'know-it-all' attitude. His suggestion that they should draw up lists of their works was rejected, as was his urgent recommendation that they travel to Italy for a few months in order to study the work of Raphael and Michelangelo on site: 'How quickly would they then be able to surpass all, so that [from then on it will be] the Italians [who would] come to Holland ...'. Although these words were an expression of Huygens' national pride, as a humanist he was nevertheless of the opinion that the path of any excellent artist had (still) to take him to Italy.

He devoted considerably more space to Jan Lievens, whom he regarded as the better portraitist and by whom he consequently had himself painted, than to Rembrandt. Like Orlers, he ascribed the greatest importance to Lievens. Nevertheless, he also recognised in Rembrandt merits which Lievens did not possess. His characterisation of Rembrandt is very precise indeed:

'Rembrandt surpasses Lievens in the faculty of penetrating to the heart of his subject matter and bringing out its essence, and his works come

The Capture of Samson, c. 1629
Wood, 61.4 x 40 cm. Bredius 489
Berlin–Dahlem, Staatliche Museen,
Gemäldegalerie

41

The Raising of Lazarus, c. 1630. Wood, 96.2 x 81.5 cm. Bredius 538
Los Angeles, County Museum of Art

Jan Lievens (1607–1674)
The Raising of Lazarus, 1631
Canvas, 103 x 112 cm
Brighton, Art Gallery and
Museum

across more vividly. ... Rembrandt ... is obsessed by the effort to translate into paint what he sees in his mind's eye, prefers smaller formats, in which he nonetheless achieves effects that you will not find in the largest works by others.'

These general comments are followed by a description of *Judas Returning the Thirty Pieces of Silver* (ill. p. 38), which Rembrandt painted in 1629. The picture was a great success at the time and very soon there were numerous copies in circulation. In Huygens' detailed and interpretative description we have rare evidence of what Rembrandt's contemporaries felt at the sight of such a picture:

'The painting of the repentant Judas returning to the high priest the pieces of silver, the price of our innocent Lord, illustrates the point I wish to make concerning all his works. It can withstand comparison with anything ever made in Italy, or for that matter with everything beautiful and admirable that has been preserved since the earliest antiquity. That single gesture of the desperate Judas - that single gesture, I say, of a raging, whining Judas grovelling for mercy he no longer hopes for or dares to show the smallest sign of expecting, his frightful visage, hair torn out of his head, his rent garment, his arms twisted, the hands clenched bloodlessly tight, fallen to his knees in a heedless outburst - that body, wholly contorted in pathetic despair, I place against all the tasteful art of all time past, and recommend to the attention of all the ignoramuses ... who hold that our age is incapable of doing or saying anything better than what has already been said or the ancients have achieved. I tell you that no one ... ever conceived, or for that matter could conceive ... that which ... a young, a born and bred Dutchman, a miller, a smooth-faced boy, has done: joining in the figure of one man so many divers particulars and expressing so many universals. Truly, my friend Rembrandt, all honour to you. To have brought Illium - even all of Asia Minor - to Italy was a lesser feat than for a Dutchman - and one who had hardly ever left his home town - to have captured for the Netherlands the trophy of artistic excellence from Greece and Italy.'

Even though he dedicates more space to Jan Lievens, Huygens finds no comparable words for him. Nor, incidentally, did the two painters take up Huygens' suggestion that they should specialise in portrait painting (Lievens) and historical paintings (Rembrandt). Rembrandt continued to include portraits in his repertoire, Lievens continued to paint historical paintings. Moreover, in the period after 1628 the painters completed several pieces on the same theme. Whether this was a conscious attempt to try their hand at a common theme and measure themselves against each other, or whether one of them wished to challenge the other, must remain pure speculation. But however similar the pictures may be in terms of composition, it is clear that Huygens' judgement is sound when he ascribes to Rembrandt the greater ability in mastering historical pictures. Works such as *The Capture of Samson* (ill. p. 40), *The Raising of Lazarus* (ill. p. 42) and *Christ on the Cross* (ill. p. 45) demonstrate powerfully the fact that Rembrandt was much more prone to dispense with the narrative in his compositions than Lievens. The language of gestures used by his figures, linked with his use of light, result in depictions full of suspense and containing portrayals of human nature. Rembrandt also succeeded in bringing atmosphere into his scenes. How much more subtle is the effect of the tranquillity of the scene in which Samson's hair is cut off as a result of the look on Delilah's face and the Philistine's expression in Rembrandt's painting than in the pointed mimicry of Lievens' figures.

The Raising of Lazarus was a theme which had been depicted frequently since the early Middle Ages. This, the final miracle before the Passion, is recounted in Chapter 11 of the Gospel according to St John. Christ goes to Mary and Martha, whose brother Lazarus has been laid to rest four days previously. He stands before the grave and calls in a loud voice, 'Lazarus, come forth. And he that was dead came forth, bound hand and foot with graveclothes: and his face was bound about with a napkin.' Traditionally, the risen man was shown already standing, but still enveloped in clothes. Those standing around the grave were often holding their noses, since the dead man was already in a state of decay.

Rembrandt and Lievens, on the other hand, painted the moment at which Lazarus returns to life. In both paintings Christ is standing with Lazarus' sisters and other mourners at the open grave from which the dead man is rising. Their pictures differ, however, in the details. In Lievens' painting Christ is standing over the grave. His hands folded and his face turned towards the heavens, he appears 'entranced'. All that is to be seen of Lazarus is his hands, which he has already lifted above the level of the grave.

In Rembrandt's version, Christ is standing directly next to the grave. The effort which he needs to reawaken the dead man is mirrored in his face. All of his strength is concentrated in his raised arm, which draws the dead man as it were magnetically from the grave. Whether the form of the pictures, which in both cases is a new design of an old theme, was elaborated jointly by Rembrandt and Lievens or whether by only one of them must remain an open question. The dates of the paintings provide no hints, since they mark only the completion and not the commencement of the works. It is not, therefore, possible to determine the originator. Rembrandt, however, knew how to use the design of the composition in such a way as to give it a much greater force of expression than that achieved by Lievens' painting. The same is true of the theme *Christ on the Cross* - by its very nature a very similar depiction - in which Rembrandt succeeds in making the suffering tangible through his choice of posture and facial expression.

At this point in their development the two painters go their separate ways. Lievens was drawn to England; Rembrandt returned to Amsterdam.

The early self-portraits

Rembrandt's self-confidence and growing artistic insight are demonstrated in the numerous self-portraits which he painted. Around thirty paintings, twenty-seven etchings and twelve drawings are known and held to be authentic. In addition, we also have the copies made by his pupils. In time, other painters painted self-portraits in the manner of Rembrandt. Rembrandt's earliest self-portraits are to be found embedded in historical pictures such as *The Stoning of St Stephen* (ill. p. 9). In painting himself thus, Rembrandt was following an old tradition, for the theory of art demanded that the artist represent himself in historical pictures since he could, in this way, more easily establish a sympathetic understanding of the emotions depicted.

Jan Lievens (1607–1674)
Christ on the Cross, 1631
Canvas, 129 x 84 cm
Nancy, Musée des Beaux–Arts

Christit on the Cross, 1631
Canvas on wood, 92.9 x 72.6 cm
Bredius–Gerson 543A
Le Mas d'Agenais, parish church

A further consideration which may have caused Rembrandt to paint himself so often was the opportunity to engage in the studies which were so imperative for portrait painting. No model could summon up as much patience as he could. In his earliest likenesses he painted himself without any particular accessories (ill. p. 8), but soon he was slipping into roles. As early as 1629, for example, he depicted himself with a *gorget*, the protective neck plate from a suit of armour (ill. p. 46). This detail also perhaps indicates that through Huygens Rembrandt had come into contact with the court in The Hague and that Frederik Hendrik had already bought pictures from him.

The Artist in his Studio (ill. p. 47) is of major importance and unique as far as the modern beholder is concerned. From this picture it is possible to gain an insight into Rembrandt's methods, which differed greatly from established procedure. In a frugally furnished room stands a huge easel, the light falling across it. Somewhat in the background, positioned well back from the easel, stands the painter regarding his picture. In his hand he holds a palette, a mahlstick and several brushes. There is no chair to

Self–portrait, c. 1629
Wood, 37.9 x 28.9 cm. Bredius 6
The Hague, Mauritshuis

suggest that he works sitting down, as was the rule at the time. We also now know that Rembrandt did not - as was usual - draw up an outline which served as a model for the completed painting, but sketched his ideas instead in brown oil paint on the ground. He subsequently built up the painting 'from front to back', which meant that the figures were completed last. Yet we can glean more than technical details from the studio portrait. The beholder - or purchaser - is only permitted to see the picture once work on it has been completed. At the moment he can only view the easel from behind; he does not know what the artist is painting. On closer inspection we see more directions, for example that a picture should hang in the correct light, just as the easel stands on a spot where it is completely lit. In addition, there should be adequate room for the beholder to view the work from the required distance, as Rembrandt is doing in his studio picture.

Words to this and similar effect have been handed down from Rembrandt himself. By painting this scene, then, he translated his principles early on into picture form whilst at the same time demonstrating that he worked without distractions and concentrated totally on the subject. It is, of course, typical of him that he felt it worthwhile to record his methods in a painting and evidence of the artist's new self-appreciation.

The Artist in his Studio, c. 1629
Wood, 25.1 x 31.9 cm. Bredius 419
Boston, Museum of Fine Arts

4   Cit. in Schwartz 1985, p. 20

5   The Holy Bible, Luke, Chapter 12, Verses 20-21, cit. in Tümpel 1986, p.31

6   Cit. in Haak 1984, p. 66

7   Alpers 1989, p. 131

8   Cit. in Schwartz 1985, p. 74-76, from which subsequent quotes are also taken

Chapter III

Rembrandt's career in Amsterdam

During the course of 1631 Rembrandt decided to go to Amsterdam. At the time it was one of the world's most affluent cities and the economic centre of the Dutch provinces. Consequently, it was beginning to attract a great many artists. With the help of the art dealer Hendrick Uylenburgh (1587-1661), Rembrandt had already sold paintings to influential Amsterdam citizens from his studio in Leiden; his name was known and he was able to reckon with a reasonably regular clientele. Hendrick Uylenburgh was a typical representative of Amsterdam's early

Johannes Elison (c. 1581–1639), 1634
Canvas, 173 x 124 cm. Bredius 200
Boston, Museum of Fine Arts

Jan Rijksen (1560/61–1637) and
Griet Jans
(c. 1560–after 1653), 1633
Canvas, 114.3 x 168.9 cm
Bredius 408
London, Buckingham Palace,
Royal Collection

capitalism. His art dealership was not limited to the sale of individual paintings; instead he worked regularly with a body of artists who handled for him the commissions which he received. With them, he also organised amateur art classes especially for children and trained apprentices. These apprentices, who had to pay for their training, were deployed largely in the production of copies of paintings in Uylenburgh's possession, which he was then able to sell at a profit. Moreover, he dealt both in etchings after paintings and in original etchings, the plates for which he likewise offered for sale. He drew up certificates and undertook the cleaning of old paintings.

Unable to set up this enterprise with his own financial resources alone, Uylenburgh had sought the backing of partners and had won the support of two very different groups of interested parties. The first of these was the artists who worked for him; with an interest in the dealership, they also shared in its profits. Secondly, he had been able to enlist the support of respected citizens with capital at their disposal. Uylenburgh's postulation that as partners they would also be the most reliable customers in respect of portrait commissions proved accurate. Their orders boosted the dealership's turnover, and this led to the distribution of higher dividends from which they then profited again. Today we would describe Uylenburgh as an entrepreneur, for his talent lay in running a profitable business with his own skill and other people's capital. Despite overstretching himself financially in the 1650s, his approach displayed model characteristics, not least in Rembrandt's eyes. Whilst still living in Leiden the artist had bought into Uylenburgh's business to the tune of 1,000 guilders. Given that in the mid-seventeenth century the weekly wage of a craftsman was 2.8 guilders, the annual income of a teacher 200 guilders and the cost of a small house in the city 300 guilders, that was a large sum.[9] Rembrandt had clearly already amassed a small fortune from his painting in Leiden. His partnership in the art dealership now meant that he was no longer reliant exclusively on the proceeds from the sale of his own pictures, but also shared in the profits of a 'commercial undertaking'. Furthermore, he was able, under Uylenburgh's aegis, to live and work in the city even before he had become a citizen of Amsterdam and - much more importantly - before becoming a member of the Guild of St Luke. Without guild membership he was debarred under city and guild law from running his own studio and attendant large-scale studio practice.

The early portraits

The Anatomy Lecture of Dr Nicolaes Tulp (1593–1674), 1632
Canvas, 169.5 x 216.5 cm
Bredius 403
The Hague, Mauritshuis

Rembrandt lived in Uylenburgh's home in *Breestraat* for three years. He had also lived in the same street during his training with Lastman. Now he began to neglect the historical painting which he had learned from Lastman in favour of the portrait commissions which he was receiving. Additionally, his work for the dealership included some teaching. His

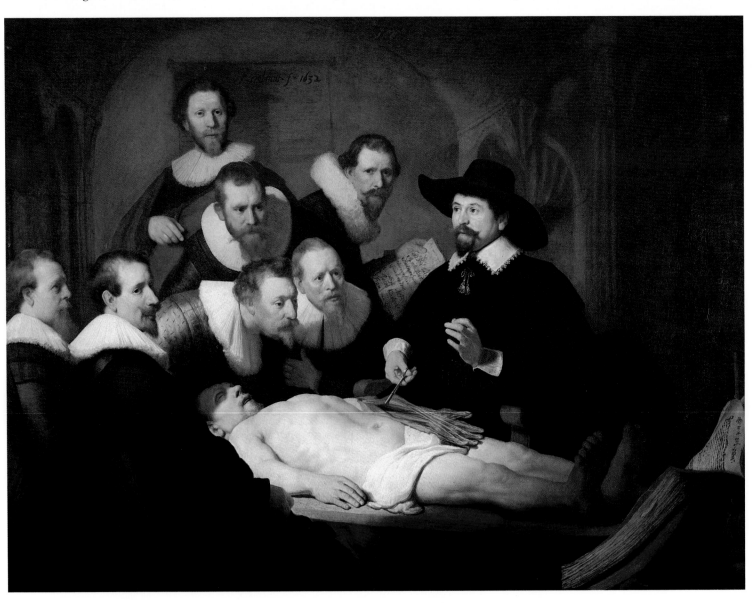

The Anatomy Lecture of Dr Johan Deyman (1620–1666), 1656
Canvas, 100 x 134 cm. Bredius 414
Amsterdam, Rijksmuseum (on
  loan from the city of Amsterdam)

most interesting commission of the year 1632 must surely have been the portrait of Dr Tulp during an anatomy lecture (ill. p. 50).

Holland had a tradition of anatomy lectures. Once a year the *Praelector Anatomiae*, the head of the surgeons' guild, would hold a public lecture for the members of his guild in the course of which the corpse of an executed criminal would be dissected. The lectures took place in the anatomical theatre, and it was common for the *Praelector* to have his portrait painted with other members on this occasion.

As head of a guild, the *Praelector* was a respected citizen and often held other offices in the city. Dr Nicolaes Tulp (1593-1674) was *Praelector* from 1628 to 1653 and subsequently burgomaster for four terms. As a famous surgeon of the day, Tulp followed in the tradition established by Andreas Vesalius (1514-1664), the first surgeon ever to dissect the bodies of animals and human beings himself and the first to successfully lay open the sinews of a hand. Tulp's own scientific success earned him the name 'Vesalius of Amsterdam'. As we shall show, Rembrandt made reference to this in his painting.

Normally, pictures depicting the anatomy lectures were group portraits in which the guild members - the *Praelector* with the corpse to be dissected in the centre - stared straight ahead out of the picture. Rembrandt's approach, on the other hand, was quite different. He took as the basis for his portrait the experience which he had gained from historical painting. The corpse lies diagonally across the picture. The protagonist, Dr Tulp, stands in the right-hand half of the picture and is just

Nicolaes Ruts (1573–1638), 1631
Wood, 116.8 x 87.3 cm. Bredius 145
New York, Frick Collection

in the process of laying open the sinews of the hand and arm, reporting on his findings as he works. With his left hand he demonstrates the finger movements which are made possible by the individual sinews. His clothes and hat mark him out as the central figure of the narrative. The guild members are grouped around the head of the corpse. Some of them are looking spellbound at the hand in which Tulp holds the scissors. Others are staring out of the picture, since Rembrandt would otherwise have had to portray them in *profil perdu*, which would have defeated the object of the commission, namely to paint a group portrait. Hence the compromise.

Despite this, Rembrandt succeeded for the first time in combining a group portrait and an action picture. In doing so, he was less concerned to produce a realistic depiction than to use the manner of the dissection to translate into picture form the comparison between Tulp and Vesalius.

As a rule, of course, dissections began with the opening up of the abdominal cavity and the brain. Only then would attention turn to the arms, which in the meantime would have been separated from the torso. Rembrandt, on the other hand, painted the corpse with the torso still intact and had Tulp begin with the arm, thereby emphasising the link

Johannes Uyttenbogaert
(1557–1646), 1633
Canvas, 132 x 102 cm. Bredius 173
Mentmore, Buckinghamshire,
collection of the Earl of Rosebery

between him and Vesalius. Rembrandt must have studied Vesalius' dissections intensively, for after his death four plaster casts of arms and legs which had been dissected by the great anatomist were found.

The painting was hung in the anatomical theatre and in 1656 was joined by a second painting by Rembrandt when the artist was commissioned to paint the portrait of Dr Tulp's successor, Dr Johan Deyman, during his anatomy lecture as well. Only a fragment of this painting (ill. p. 51) has survived, having been severely damaged in a fire in the anatomical theatre in 1723. However, its composition is known to us from a sketch which Rembrandt made for its immense architectonic picture frame. In this second anatomy picture the corpse and anatomist are placed in the centre; the other guild members stand to the left and right of this group, but are clearly also - as in the earlier portrait - closely involved in the action. The corpse rises up into the picture head-on, with the result that the body appears greatly foreshortened. The position is reminiscent of the depiction by Andrea Mantegna (1431-1506) of the dead Christ; Rembrandt even borrowed the cloth which here covers the lower half of the body. Because of the positioning of the corpse, the beholder has a view into the opened abdominal cavity. Deyman is in the process of dissecting the brain; the university lecturer Gysbrecht Calkoen on his left holds the skull-cap in his hand.

In this picture, painted more than twenty years later, Rembrandt

*Cornelis Claesz. Anslo (1592–1646)
and his wife Aeltje Gerritsdr.
Schouten (1598–1657)*, 1641
Canvas, 176 x 210 cm. Bredius 409
Berlin–Dahlem, Staatliche Museen,
Gemäldegalerie

adheres more closely to reality. He shows the exact order in which the dissection takes place. Yet here too he combines a group portrait with the form of a historical picture. From the trouble he takes to produce an exact representation of the dissected parts of the body in both pictures we can discern his great interest in the human body.

Rembrandt scored a huge success in Amsterdam with his portraits. His insistence on moving on from the accepted form of portraiture and adopting the form of a historical painting, as seen for the first time in *The Anatomy Lecture of Dr Nicolaes Tulp*, also extended to several other commissions. In 1633, for example, he painted the portrait of *Jan Rijksen and Griet Jans* (ill. p. 49). Jan Rijksen was a master shipbuilder and shareholder in the Dutch East Indies Company and it has been shown that in 1620 at least he was its major shipbuilder. Rembrandt depicts him at his desk as he completes a workshop drawing. On the table lie several papers and writing and drawing utensils. Rijksen holds in his hand the compass which he has just been using. The light shines through the window onto the drawing. In order that he might depict the customer *en face* and also incorporate the latter's wife, Rembrandt has the wife enter through the door with a letter in her hand. The shipbuilder turns and takes the letter, but does not look at its deliverer. He fixes instead on a point outside the picture. His wife, in her inferior position, is aware that her disturbance is disagreeable. She keeps her hand on the door handle and quickly hands over the letter.

Here, then, Rembrandt portrays the subjects of the portrait at their various work or tasks. Both are busy. Even during this brief meeting they do not initiate any contact, nor do they have any relationship with the beholder; each is absorbed in his or her own activities.

The double portrait naturally offered greater opportunities for such an approach than the individual portrait. In 1641 Rembrandt painted the Mennonite preacher Cornelis Claesz. Anslo and his wife (ill. p. 54). The lay preacher, whose main occupation was that of a textile and carpet trader, evidently set great store on having both aspects of his life recorded in the picture. Expensively dressed, he sits behind his desk. On this lies a carpet, as was usual in Holland at the time. A second appears to have been thrown carelessly over the first. It hangs down at the side, so that the pattern can be discerned, and forms heavy folds, emphasising the exclusiveness and quality of the material. In addition to this carpet, an allusion to Anslo's occupation, there are several books lying on the table. On the lectern, towering above the rest, is an opened Bible. In the background it is possible to discern a shelf containing more volumes. Clearly the lay preacher, who in the picture is concerned largely with interpreting the Bible, is an educated man. On the right in the foreground sits Anslo's wife listening to her husband, who has turned to her and is speaking urgently to her. Yet here too there is no eye contact. Although he has turned towards his wife, she is not looking at him, but gazing into the void.

Rijksen was a Catholic, Anslo a Mennonite. Nicolaes Ruts, whom Rembrandt had painted in 1631 (ill. p. 52), although born into a Mennonite family, had gone over to the Reformed Church with its Calvinist tendencies. Another Calvinist customer was the English pastor Johannes Elison (ill. p. 48), whose portrait was painted in 1634. A year earlier Rembrandt had painted Johannes Uyttenbogaert, the originator of the 'remonstrance' (ill. p. 53; see p. 11) and thus an opponent of the Calvinists. Many more examples could be given which prove that the artist did not receive his commissions from the members of one particular faith. He was not a follower of either side. His customers were, however, all members of the bourgeoisie. Occasionally he got the opportunity to paint a government official at the beginning of his career, but in general the patricians preferred the classical courtly style which had originated in France and was slowly becoming established in Holland too. Thus although Rembrandt painted the portraits of four future burgomasters of Amsterdam, he did so long before they had achieved this particular height in their career.

Although Rembrandt did not succeed in firing the enthusiasm of the city's patricians for his style of painting, his portraits nevertheless brought him a great deal of success in Amsterdam. His habit of incorporating action of some kind and of drawing out different levels of meaning through the use of chiaroscuro made an impression. He was not only overwhelmed with commissions, but also copied fervently. Accordingly, in 1634 Rembrandt saw an opportunity to set up on his own as a master

Self–portrait, 1633
Wood, 55 x 46 cm. Bredius 23
Berlin–Dahlem, Staatliche Museen,
Gemäldegalerie

Saskia, 1633
Wood, 52.5 x 44.5 cm. Bredius 97
Dresden, Staatliche
Kunstsammlungen,
Gemäldegalerie

painter. He joined the Guild of St Luke, moved into a studio and began to run his own practice. In the process, he adopted many of the principles on which his mentor of many years, Uylenburgh, worked. In 1634 he was married to Saskia Uylenburgh, whom he had met through Uylenburgh a year previously.

Saskia: wife and model

Saskia Uylenburgh came from Friesland. Her father, Rombertus Uylenburgh (?-1624), was one of the most influential men in the government there and burgomaster of Leeuwarden. His name is often linked with that of William of Orange, who was assassinated immediately after a meeting with Rombertus. Saskia was born on 2 August 1612. Just six years later she lost her mother; by 1624 she was an orphan. It is unclear whether she lived with various relatives in turn in the years which followed and first came to Amsterdam in 1633 or whether she was taken into the household of her cousin Aaltje, who was married to the famous reformed pastor Johannes Cornelisz. Sylvius (1564-1638), in 1624. We can, however, assume that Saskia and Rembrandt met at the home of her first cousin, the art dealer Hendrick Uylenburgh.

The earliest portraits of Saskia were painted in 1633. Whether she and Rembrandt were just getting to know each other at this point or whether Rembrandt had the opportunity to paint his young fiancée only after their engagement must also remain an open question. They were married on 2 July 1634 in Friesland.

In marrying Saskia, Rembrandt had not only married above his station but had also become a wealthy man, for Saskia brought into the marriage an appreciable inheritance. This inheritance enabled Rembrandt to live in prosperity, and in the final analysis it was almost certainly this which seduced him into buying a large house in *Antonisbreestraat* in 1639. It also brought with it irritation from Saskia's relatives. In 1638 he instituted legal proceedings against these relatives for claiming that Saskia was dissipating her fortune on pomp and frittering it away. He did not run into serious trouble, however, until after Saskia's death in June 1642, but was able to keep his creditors, including relatives of his wife, at bay.

In the eight years of their marriage Saskia bore four children, of whom only the youngest son, Titus (1641-1668) survived. The first son, Rombertus, and the two daughters, both named Cornelia, lived only a few weeks. Saskia did not recover from the birth of her son Titus. On 14 June 1642 she too died. Titus was just 9 months old.

Rembrandt painted and drew Saskia frequently. Among his drawings there are even studies of Saskia in the domestic sphere, for example sleeping or with an infant in her arms. This is never the case in the paintings. Before their wedding Rembrandt had painted several very different portraits of her. She appears most formal in the painting *Saskia with a Veil* (ill. p. 60) from 1633. The young woman is set diagonally in an oval frame, has her head slightly turned and is looking straight towards the beholder. She betrays not the least emotion. Even the play of light and shadow on her face does not obviate the portrait's lack of expression.

In another, equally small but rectangular painting from the same year Rembrandt gave his wife much more lively features (ill. p. 56). Here Saskia is wearing a large feather hat. She has turned her head so severely that she is staring out of the picture. Her smile causes her face to wrinkle,

Previous page:
Saskia in a Rich Costume with a Large Flat Hat, c. 1634
Wood, 99.5 x 78.8 cm. Bredius 101
Kassel, Staatliche Kunstsammlungen, Gemäldegalerie

Saskia as Flora, 1634
Canvas, 125 x 101 cm. Bredius 102
Leningrad, Hermitage

Saskia as Flora, 1635
Canvas, 123.5 x 97.5 cm
Bredius 103
London, National Gallery

her eyes are narrowed and framed by laughter lines. The wide brim of the hat leaves the forehead and part of the eyes in shadow, whereas light is falling across the lower half of the face, the neck and shoulders. With this turning of the head and the smile, Rembrandt succeeds in suggesting vivacity. One has the impression from this picture that he had now become familiar with his wife's facial features and bearing. It is one of the few genuine portraits of Saskia in which Rembrandt does not merely render her facial features, but also endeavours to represent her character. In the other portraits of her which he painted there is no trace of the structure of her personality. Instead, the impression which they give is that Rembrandt had finally found a live model for his female figures.

Before his engagement Rembrandt had rarely painted women and then mostly - apart from the commissioned portraits - old women. Now he did numerous paintings in which he transformed his wife, just as he portrayed himself in a variety of roles. In 1634 he painted her in a lavish costume and with a large flat hat (ill. p. 57). The upper part of the body (not merely the shoulders) is once again painted three-quarters on, the head this time turned into the picture so that the face is seen only in profile. This pose, in which Saskia turns away from the beholder, conveys the

Saskia with a Veil, 1633
Wood, 65 x 48 cm. Bredius 94
Amsterdam, Rijksmuseum

*Rembrandt and Saskia in the
Scene: the Prodigal Son in
a Bordello*, 1635–1636
Canvas, 161 x 131 cm. Bredius 30
Dresden, Staatliche
Kunstsammlungen,
Gemäldegalerie

haughtiness of an elegantly dressed woman. The sumptuously ornamented dress is partly covered by a fur thrown carelessly over the shoulders. Arm, neck, ear and hair are adorned with gold, which glitters in the light.

It was certainly not Rembrandt's wish to emphasise his wife's wealth in this painting or indeed to give the impression of haughtiness. What he wanted was to represent an elegant and wealthy lady. Saskia was simply his model. From X-rays we know that Saskia first held a dagger in her hand and that Rembrandt had therefore originally planned a representation of Lucrezia. The change of plan had nothing to do with the model.

Rembrandt depicted his wife in the most varied - and not always positive - roles. She was available and - as his female counterpart - came closest to meeting the requirement that a painter should depict himself in his histories in order that he might express the maximum possible emotion. Rembrandt conformed, albeit only to a certain extent, to that view. Besides, at the time a model was not necessarily identified with the role into which he or she slipped for a historical painting. There are even examples of women of rank 'being depicted as naked or half-naked figures in historicised portraits'.[10] To what extent Rembrandt stepped outside the rules in force during the seventeenth century is something to which we will return.

Saskia sat for the figure of *Flora* many times. In 1634 Rembrandt painted the goddess still as a young girl (ill. p. 58). In front of a tangle of trees, bushes and thicket which merely shine from out of the darkness of a wood stands the brightly lit figure of a young woman with flowers in her hair. In her right hand she is holding a staff enwreathed in flowers; her left hand is held in front of her body. The tucked-up dress adds a theatrical touch.

In the *Flora* (ill. p. 59) from 1635, a year later, Saskia is a fine figure of a woman. At this time she was pregnant with her first child, which explains why her face appears much fuller than in the earlier likenesses. Yet Rembrandt could, surely, hardly have wanted to play on the pregnancy in this Flora. In fact, he originally conceived the picture as *Judith with the Head of Holofernes*. The hand which now holds the spray of flowers still holds the bloody head of Holofernes in the X-ray. Once again we are confronted with a change of plan which could be interpreted as consideration for Saskia, although by interpreting the changes in this way we are, under the circumstances, imputing to the painter our own notions of morality. Nevertheless, analysis of the painting *The Prodigal Son in a Bordello* (ill. p. 61) has been based largely on a historical assumptions of this kind. For a long time this painting was regarded as a double portrait and gave cause for speculation about the marriage. Although it was first interpreted in 1925 as a historical picture on the theme of the prodigal son, it was not until the beginning of the 1970s that this interpretation of the picture was finally accepted.

In a room identifiable as a tavern from the half-seen board in the top left-hand corner, on which the landlord has chalked the bill, a young man sits in elegant but dowdy attire at a richly laden table. Laughing, he turns his head backwards, that is out of the picture, and raises his glass. His left hand rests suggestively on the hips of the young woman seated on his lap. This figure, whom we see from the back, also has her head turned and is smiling enigmatically at the beholder. A modern X-ray has shown that the painting was previously rectangular and that in the background,

Maurits Huygens
(1595–1642), 1632
Wood, 31.2 x 24.6 cm. Bredius 161
Hamburg, Kunsthalle

between Saskia and Rembrandt, a naked lute player indicated the depravity of the place. She was painted over with the peacock's feathers which are visible behind Rembrandt's head.

Why Rembrandt cut the picture down and eliminated the lute player is not known. Possibly it was part and parcel of his attempts to reduce histories to their basic content and to eliminate any distracting, but explanatory, embellishment. Nevertheless, the picture remained a history. Saskia and Rembrandt were merely models, and the picture was not intended to reflect an outlook on life which embraced a love of show, ostentation and extravagance.

During those first few years in Amsterdam Rembrandt - against the advice of Constantijn Huygens - mainly painted portraits. As we have seen, his success lay in applying the principles of historical painting to the painting of likenesses. Now he began once again to turn his attention to history.

Yet the use of living models in his pictures still fascinated him. He was more familiar with Saskia and himself than with others and it was for this reason that he used his wife in his work. He did not paint her - as other artists painted their wives - in a domestic family atmosphere, but drew her into his studio work. This was one of the principles which differentiated him from other artists of the age.

Jakob de Gheyn III
(1596–1641), 1632
Wood, 29.9 x 24.5 cm. Bredius 162
London, Dulwich College Gallery

Rembrandt's pictures for the court in The Hague

Rembrandt was one of a small circle of Dutch painters who succeeded in winning commissions from the court in The Hague. Reigning there as stadtholder since 1625 was Frederik Hendrik, a son of William and half-brother of Maurits (cf. p. 15). Maurits had concentrated primarily on the building of fortifications. Frederik Hendrik, who had been brought up in France and - as a godson of Henry IV of France (1553-1610) - had had contact with the French court, concentrated on the artistic development of The Hague. He had several palaces built in and around the city and also saw to their decor and furnishing. For this he summoned the best architects and painters in the Netherlands to court.

Frederik Hendrik's position was anything but easy, for he was not even the highest-ranking nobleman in The Hague. A plan to confer upon William of Orange the hereditary title of Earl of Holland and attendant privileges had been thwarted by his assassination. Thus the Princes of Orange and Nassau continued to reign as so-called stadtholders. It was under Frederik Hendrik that this office first became hereditary.

However, Frederick V, prince-elector of the Palatinate (1596-1632), and his wife Elizabeth Stuart, daughter of James I of England, still resided in The Hague. Frederick had unsuccessfully reigned over Bohemia for a year and as a relative of the House of Orange had settled in the city in

The Raising of the Cross, c. 1633. Canvas, 96.2 x 72.2 cm. Bredius 548. Munich, Alte Pinakothek

The Raising of the Cross, c. 1633
Detail

Peter Paul Rubens (1577–1640)
The Raising of the Cross,
1610–1611
Middle panel of a triptych
Wood, 462 x 341 cm
Antwerp, cathedral

1621. The Dutch mockingly called him the 'Winter King'. He and his wife presided over a splendid court run on French lines. Together they set the tone in The Hague - including in matters of art.

Frederik Hendrik, who in 1625 was married to one of Elizabeth's ladies-in-waiting, Amalia van Solms (1602-1675), clearly felt compelled to compete with Frederick and Elizabeth. The rivalry affected both the way in which he ran his household and his promotion of the arts. Gerrit van Honthorst (1590-1656), for example, worked first for the Winter King before becoming court painter in the court of Frederik Hendrik.

The stadtholder's adviser as he built up his collection of paintings was his secretary, the aforementioned Constantijn Huygens, who as a result of his acquaintance with Rembrandt was able to establish contact between the stadtholder and the artist. Lievens too received commissions from the court.

The court's first purchases may have been made whilst Rembrandt was still in Leiden. As one of them was a self-portrait of the artist, it is reasonable to assume that not all were commissions, but that a few finished paintings from the artist's studio were also selected. Frederik

65

Peter Paul Rubens (1577–1640)
The Descent from the Cross, 1612
Middle panel of a triptych
Wood, 420 x 360 cm
Antwerp, cathedral

*The Descent from
the Cross*, c. 1633
Wood, 89.4 x 65.2 cm. Bredius 550
Munich, Alte Pinakothek

Hendrik used some of them as gifts to the English court. Unfortunately, it is no longer possible to determine the exact timing of the purchase of these pictures. In 1632 Rembrandt received his first firm commissions from the court, although possibly not yet through the good services of Huygens, since the stadtholder's secretary preferred Jan Lievens as a portraitist.

In 1632 the stadtholder ordered a painting of Amalia van Solms (ill. p. 69) as a counterpart to his own portrait, which Gerrit van Honthorst had painted in 1631 (ill. p. 68). Despite opinion to the contrary, Rembrandt must have been in The Hague at that time in order to be able to complete this commission. This view is supported by the fact that he must have studied Frederik Hendrik's likeness closely, since he borrowed from this the false frame which Honthorst had created in his painting. For this portrait Rembrandt observed convention. Amalia van Solms is rendered in profile so that she is looking at her counterpart, the stadtholder. Above all, however, the painting is fully lit. Rembrandt dispenses here with his chiaroscuro effect and adapts to the courtly style.

During his stay in The Hague Rembrandt evidently received several commissions, both from courtiers and from the good burghers of the

Gerard van Honthorst (1590–1656)
Frederik Hendrik
(1583–1647), 1631
Canvas, 77 x 61 cm
The Hague, Huis ten Bosch

city, since all these portraits are dated 1632. The most interesting are the two pictures which he painted for Maurits Huygens (1595-1642) and Jakob de Gheyn the Younger (1596-1641). Maurits Huygens had taken over the post of secretary to the Council of State from his father, just as his brother Constantijn had taken over that of secretary to the stadtholder. As the son of the court artist of the same name, the painter Jakob de Gheyn the Younger had also grown up in The Hague and was a close friend and contemporary of Maurits Huygens. In 1632 both had their portraits painted by Rembrandt (ill. p. 62 and 63). Rembrandt set each of the men at a slant so that their bodies are turned toward each other. He turned their heads, however, in such a way that they stare almost straight ahead and out of the paintings. The outer half of each face is fully lit, the inner half slightly shadowed. In this way Rembrandt ensured that the paintings were taken as counterparts if viewed together, but could also exist independently. This evidently fulfilled the wishes of his customers, for the related paintings are an interesting record of the friendship between the two men. Conceived as a pair, the pictures remained in the possession of the two subjects until de Gheyn's death. As had obviously been agreed, Maurits Huygens inherited his friend's picture. For over 120 years they then remained together before being separated once again when they were sold.

*Amalia van Solms
(1602–1675)*, 1632
Canvas, 68.5 x 55.5 cm. Bredius 99
Paris, Musée Jacquemart–André

Jakob de Gheyn owned two more paintings by Rembrandt, one of them the aforementioned *Peter and Paul in Conversation* (ill. p. 30). In all probability it was his idea to commission the memorable double portrait from Rembrandt. It is likely, however, that the artist's most important commission for the court - the five Passion pictures painted for Frederik Hendrik - was commissioned as a result of the patronage of Constantijn Huygens, and as these were historical pictures, Huygens would certainly have been able to justify the award of the commission to Rembrandt. Rembrandt was to paint *The Raising of the Cross, The Descent from the Cross, The Entombment of Christ, The Resurrection* and *The Ascension of Christ*. In the 1640s the stadtholder also ordered *The Adoration of the Shepherds* and the *Circumcision* in the same format.

The commission is interesting because it is mentioned in Rembrandt's (only surviving) letters, from which we can assess his attitude to his customers. In this case it was six years before he had finally completed the last picture. *The Raising of the Cross* and *The Descent from the Cross* were finished by 1633 or 1634. Rembrandt had chosen as a model the two large middle panels of the triptychs which Rubens had painted for churches in Antwerp in 1610 or 1612 (ill. p. 65 and 67).

In both pictures we can once again discern the methods which

Rembrandt had developed during his Leiden period for the painting of historical pictures. For one thing, he concentrated on the main characters. Anything which might, in his view, have interfered with any direct feeling of sympathy was eliminated or banished to the shadowed zones of the picture. Thus in *The Raising of the Cross* (ill. p. 64) the body of Christ is bathed in bright light. A shimmer of light falls too across the armour worn by the executioner raising the cross. A second executioner - with Rembrandt's face - contributes towards the effect. He is also just within the glimmer of light. A weak reflection falls upon the captain, who is to be found further back and on a horse. In contrast, the other figures, including the thieves crucified with Christ, who are just being led past in the background, are not clearly distinguishable or identifiable.

Although in *The Descent from the Cross* (ill. p. 66) the background is illuminated and it is possible to make out bushes and a building in the city, thus indicating the setting (before the city gates), it is once again only Christ, the cross and the men helping who are bathed in light. As in Rubens' paintings, the corpse is lowered from the cross with the help of a cloth on which traces of the nailing and the crown of thorns are still visible in the form of blood-red stigmata. But in the Rubens the helpers and the grieving women frame the dead Christ and it is the action of the living which is emphasised first and foremost. In the Rembrandt the shroud is the foil against which the carefully lowered body becomes visible. No action is depicted here, only love of the dead Christ and sympathy, as expressed above all by the young man (John?) receiving the body. This man, who, deeply grieved, is pressing his head against Christ's body whilst his arms hold the body under the cloth, bears the artist's features. He is shown in a similar position to that which he occupied in *The Raising of the Cross*, but this time not as an executioner, ready and willing to carry out a death sentence, but as a man suffering and displaying compassion.

Though Rembrandt has placed the grieving women - part of the action in the Rubens - in the lower left-hand corner of the picture, they are nevertheless not part of what is happening. They are mentioned only 'on the margins'; witness the fact that they have been much more obviously relegated to the shadowed zone than the two old people in the background and are barely recognisable. *The Descent from the Cross* shows more clearly than *The Raising of the Cross* just how closely Rembrandt stuck to the formal construction of his model whilst at the same time imparting a completely different overall impression through his different emphasis.

Both paintings must have been delivered soon after their completion. Three years later, in 1636, Rembrandt wrote to Constantijn Huygens saying that he was working fervently and that the *Ascension* was ready and the other two pictures half-finished. In the letter he enquires whether he should deliver all of the pictures at the same time or the *Ascension* in advance. In a second letter he is clearly reacting to a (no longer surviving) letter from Huygens in which the latter confirms the arrival of the *Ascension*. In this letter he endeavours to double the agreed price of the picture (600 guilders) and offers the advice that 'the best place to show it is the gallery of His Excellency since there is a strong light there'.[11] This sentence demonstrates, as does his assurance that he will soon be coming to The Hague, how important it was to the artist that his pictures were positioned in accordance with his own ideas and also that he placed the greatest store on their being presented in the right light.

The Ascension of Christ, 1636
Canvas, 92.7 x 68.3 cm
Bredius 557
Munich, Alte Pinakothek

The *Ascension* (ill. p. 70) is divided into an earthly and a heavenly sector. In the lower part, in the shadow of the clouds, the astonished apostles watch the miracle. The faint light enables us to see only a few faces. Christ, on a white cloud and accompanied by putti, floats into the light, where he is received by a garland of rays in which hovers a dove representing the Holy Spirit. The original representation of God the Father which this painting contained was almost certainly painted over by Rembrandt for religious reasons, since the Calvinists could not countenance the depiction of God. This painting is far more conventional in its construction than the first two and almost certainly caused disappointment at court. After its delivery Rembrandt allowed another three years to elapse.

In 1639 Rembrandt signed the contract for the house in *Breestraat*, for which he was to pay 13,000 guilders. A deposit of 1,200 guilders became due immediately. This money appears not to have been at Rembrandt's disposal, despite the fortune which Saskia had brought into the marriage - a sum of around 40,000 guilders. Consequently, he was now in a hurry to collect the rest of his fee from the stadtholder. Once again he wrote a letter to Huygens, in which he explained why he had waited so long with the pictures and spoke of 'great zeal and devotion', 'studious application' and, above all, of his belief that 'in these two pictures ... the greatest and most natural emotion has been expressed, which is also the main reason why they have taken so long to execute'.[12] In order to put Huygens in a gracious frame of mind, Rembrandt promised him a picture, evidently *The Blinding of Samson*, a large and valuable historical picture.

Rembrandt was clearly in such difficulty that he spared neither trouble nor money to raise the 1,200 guilders. Although Huygens declined the offer of a gift, Rembrandt sent it to him regardless. The letters which followed were concerned exclusively with payment for the commission. He tried again to raise the price, albeit without success. In addition, he suggested that the money should be delivered to him directly through the tax collector in Amsterdam. When payment did not follow promptly he sent a reminder. The frenzy to which he succumbed in order to get the money evidently also accompanied him whilst painting. For years the paintings had stood half-finished in his studio; now they had to be completed with all speed.

The first letter from 1639, when he announced their completion, appears not to have been altogether honest, for Rembrandt clearly packed the pictures wet. This resulted in the paint layers never binding and explains their present poor condition. *The Resurrection* (ill. p. 74) was restored as early as 1755. Afterwards the restorer left an unusual inscription on the back: 'Rimbrand Creavit me. P. H. Brinkmann resuscitavit Te/1755' (Rembrandt created me. P. H. Brinkmann brought you back to life/1755).[13] Adding to the Passion series in 1646, Rembrandt delivered to the court *The Adoration of the Shepherds* (ill. p. 131) and the *Circumcision* (destroyed). This time he received the required sum of 1,200 guilders. Involved in the decoration of the stadtholder's palaces there were, however, artists who imitated the style which was fashionable in France. Here they had no use for Rembrandt's paintings.

It may be, of course, that Rembrandt's style was not the only reason for his fall from favour. Through the letters it had become clear how unreliably Rembrandt worked at certain times. The stadtholder had had to wait six years for the completion of a commission for five pictures.

The Entombment of Christ, 1639
Canvas, 92.5 x 68.9 cm
Bredius 560
Munich, Alte Pinakothek

What is more, repeated attempts to raise the agreed price could certainly not have increased the artist's popularity.

We will return to look in detail at Rembrandt's financial situation later. His behaviour, surprisingly well documented concerning this commission, must however have prevented many potential customers from becoming involved with him.

Mythological themes

Rembrandt painted only a few histories with themes from classical mythology. In this respect he was in line with his contemporaries; it was not, as has so often and so variously been claimed, indicative of his lack of a humanist education. During the sixteenth century the classical authors, common property in Renaissance Italy, were translated into and published in a variety of languages in order to make them accessible to a wider public. Their works were illustrated with wood-engravings which painters were then able to use as models. For all that, such themes were taken up only hesitantly.

Whilst still in Leiden Rembrandt had painted an *Andromeda* (ill. p. 34) - we can even identify the model (cf. p. 35) - and a *Tale* (ill. p. 10) which despite several attempts remains uninterpreted to this day. He also worked on mythological themes in Amsterdam, albeit only rarely: Saskia served as his model for the aforementioned depictions of *Flora* (ill. p. 58 and 59), and a depiction of *Minerva* from 1632 actually appears to have been a portrait commission from The Hague. Nor are these examples, which could just as easily be classified as *portraits histories*, unique; Rembrandt also painted other histories with mythological themes. However, since he tended, as in his biblical representations, either to omit attributes which were necessary to the identification of a scene or to incorporate them in such a way as to make them barely recognisable as such, researchers have had particular difficulty in interpreting two pictures from 1634 and 1636. The earlier of the two is *Artemisia Receiving her Husband's Ashes Mixed with Wine* from 1634 (ill. p. 76), which in the course of time has been given various titles. Until recently the favoured title was *Sophonisba Receiving the Poisoned Cup*. The Numidian queen Sophonisba was captured during Rome's war against Carthage by Rome's ally Massinissa, whom she asked to protect her from the Romans. The Romans demanded that she be handed over, and Massinissa was unable to resist. He therefore sent to her a servant with a poisoned cup and a message reminding her that she had asked him to slay her rather than deliver her up to the Romans, whereupon Sophonisba took the cup and emptied it.

The alternative subject of the painting is Artemisia, the wife of Mausolus, who was responsible for the building of the Mausoleum - one of the seven wonders of the world - which she erected as a sepulchre for her husband following his death. Artemisia also wanted to serve as a grave for her husband's body herself and so drank his ashes mixed with wine.

Differences in the features traditionally found in representations of the Artemisia and Sophonisba themes in Rembrandt's day, especially the man in the background holding a sack from which the ashes are shaken into the cup, have led Tümpel to identify the painting with the Artemisia theme. Before the splendidly dressed queen stands the hand-

The Resurrection, 1639
Canvas on wood, 91.9 x 67 cm
Bredius 561
Munich, Alte Pinakothek

Artemisia Receiving her Husband's Ashes Mixed with Wine, 1634
Canvas, 142 x 153 cm. Bredius 468
Madrid, Prado

maiden with the filled cup, which she offers like a sacred object, not in her bare hands but in a cloth. Artemisia has laid her hand on her stomach and in doing so points to Mausolus' grave. The man with the sack of ashes has already carried out his function and is disappearing into the background. The sack, which he still has open, is barely visible on reproductions.

Here, once again, Rembrandt uses the methods which he had developed in Leiden. He seizes upon a thrilling moment in the story and does not go into what has gone before, or only does so by way of allusion. It is this which often makes identification so difficult. What it also demonstrates, however, is that Rembrandt studied intensively the themes which he tackled. Such study necessarily requires the intellectual abilities which it is often denied that he had. We will come back to this point when we look at Rembrandt's biblical histories.

Researchers have encountered similar difficulty in interpreting a picture from 1636 (ill. p. 78) which shows a naked female figure lying on a bed. A curtain which closes off the room behind the bed is being drawn back by a handmaiden. Models for this picture are to be found not only in classical mythology, but also in biblical stories from the Old Testament. The choice of theme is limited somewhat by the fact that the half-sitting woman is clearly expecting someone. Twelve different interpretations have been suggested for the painting. Although scholars have been agreed since 1933 on Erwin Panofsky's interpretation - that the picture is of *Danaë*, to whom Zeus comes as a shower of gold - Gary Schwartz has recently linked the picture with the story of *Aegina Visited by Jupiter in the Form of Fire*.

Both stories concern the transformation of the same great god in order that he might approach a mortal woman. As a result, Danaë bore Perseus

*The Goddess Diana Bathing,
with the Stories of Actaeon
and Callisto,* 1634
Canvas, 73.5 x 93.5 cm
Bredius 472
Isselburg, Schloß Anholt,
collection of the Prince
of Salm–Salm

and Aegina Aeacus, two of Zeus' many children, who were classed as demigods.

At the root of this problem of identification lies the absence of the figure of the god. Rembrandt painted neither the fire into which the god was transformed when he visited Aegina nor the shower of gold which would prove the Danaë theory. The golden shimmer on the female figure's skin which also shines throughout the entire room was interpreted by Panofsky as a hint at the shower of gold. But this golden light could also be the reflection of a fire, as Schwartz claims. Even the chained boy who decorates the head of the bed and represents Anterus, the symbol of godly love, offers no help in identifying the picture. Only the argument that the story of Danaë was a traditional theme but that the story of Aegina was not may be seen as a pointer to the female figure's identification with Danaë.

The similarity between these two mythological tales and the absence of the god in his adopted form thus make it difficult for today's beholder to decide in favour of one or the other theme. The question is also raised as to whether this knowledge would be of great interest. What is surely important is the manner in which Rembrandt solved the problem of depicting the secret love of a mortal for a god. He emphasises the beauty of the naked figure, sets her in a bright but soft light which shines so intensely that it spreads throughout the room and bathes it in gold. The

Danaë, or Aegina Visited by
Jupiter in the Form of Fire, 1636
Canvas, 185 x 203 cm. Bredius 474
Leningrad, Hermitage

furnishings and their increased splendour as a result of the light reflect the splendour of the moment.

Rembrandt's other illustrations of stories from classical mythology are not accompanied by problems of identification. For all that, they often brim with many layers of significance which are not intelligible at first glance. His *Ganymede* from 1635 (ill. p. 80) does not depict a beautiful boy being carried off by Zeus in the form of an eagle, but a sobbing, fat child who in his fear is no longer able to control himself. Interpretation of the painting as a parody of the ancient world ignores the point made by Karel van Mander in his *Schilderboek (Lives of Painters*, cf. Chapter I, p. 15), a priceless source of information for Rembrandt, that Ganymede is one and the same as Aquarius, a sign of the zodiac, and thus brings rain. Rembrandt draws our attention to this by painting the boy 'having a tinkle'.

Yet there is another reason for the representation of Ganymede as a small child. The innocent souls of the dead, which God plucks from the mortal hell of man and takes unto himself, have been represented as small children since the Middle Ages. During the Renaissance the neo-Platonists linked this with the Ganymede myth. The death of a child was equated with the abduction of Ganymede by Zeus. These components are all contained in Rembrandt's picture. Clearly, detailed knowledge is often a prerequisite for understanding his pictures.

The inventory which was drawn up on Rembrandt's insolvency lists twenty-four books, including a Bible, a German edition of Flavius Josephus and Dürer's book on proportions. The titles of most of the others are not given, but it is safe to assume that Karel van Mander's *Schilderboek (Lives of Painters)* was among them. In addition, Rembrandt owned engravings and etchings after the works of Dutch, Flemish, Italian and German masters. In order to design his histories as he did he needed not only written sources but also pictures. Both together enabled him to create designs which were new but nevertheless based closely enough on models for them to remain comprehensible to his contemporaries (although not necessarily to later generations). The manner in which he appropriated and elaborated certain themes for his own use often made his pictures incomprehensible in later centuries and gave rise to the preconceptions and false interpretations which we have already mentioned.

The biblical histories

Between 1633 and 1640, Rembrandt's first few years in Amsterdam, the artist's fame as a portraitist grew. At the same time he also became a court painter to the stadtholder Frederik Hendrik. For all that, he did not limit himself during these years to the painting of portraits commissioned by the rich citizens of Amsterdam and pictures for the court. In addition to his pictures of Saskia and a few mythological paintings, he also worked on biblical histories, to which he obviously devoted a great deal of time.

Like the paintings with mythological themes, Rembrandt painted these pictures uncommissioned. They were destined for sale on the open market and often stood for years in the studio before a buyer was found for them. It may be that Frederik Hendrik's commissioning of the Passion series caused Rembrandt once again to take a greater interest in such histories, but without doubt other motives also came into play.

The Church was no longer a potential purchaser of biblical scenes, but members of the bourgeoisie began to build themselves large houses and to buy up palaces formerly owned by the aristocracy, which they turned into country seats. The large rooms could not be filled exclusively with portraits. In order to prove his piety, therefore, a Calvinist could justify the purchase of pictures which took as their theme the life of Christ. Accordingly, these pictures were expected to express inner communion, revelation or compassion.

The demand for such pictures was undoubtedly one of the reasons why Rembrandt turned once again to historical painting. But in addition to the small-format pictures so typical of his Leiden period, he now also dared to tackle larger canvases. The earliest example is *Christ in the Storm on the Sea of Genezareth* from 1633 (ill. p. 83).

The picture is based on an event which is recounted in Chapter 4 of the Gospel according to St Mark. Throughout the day Christ has been telling the people parables from a boat on the Sea of Genezareth. In the evening he travels across the sea to the other bank with his disciples. Once they are at sea a great storm blows up, which grips the disciples with terror and panic. They wake the sleeping Jesus, who calms the wind

and the waves with a few words and then says to them, 'Why are thee so fearful? how is it that ye have no faith?'

In his picture Rembrandt fuses two moments from the story into one scene. The boat is being lifted by a huge wave. Several of the disciples are in the process of reefing the sails so that they do not founder. One has been seasick and is leaning over the railing. Two are flinging themselves at Jesus and waking him. Yet already a ray of light is breaking through the clouds; the sky is opening up. Behind the boat the sea is becoming calm, and the helmsman behind Jesus has regained control of his rudder. The moment of great terror and the calming are depicted simultaneously. In the front half of the boat the disciples are fighting for their lives, whilst Christ is already posing the question as to their faith.

In this picture Rembrandt wanted to depict fear and unbelief as well as the revelation that true faith brings salvation and redemption. Sea and sky form the ship's backdrop. Because of its size, it appears to be unavoidably at the mercy of the elements. The fearful, unbelieving disciples do not see the light which brings salvation. The presence of Christ and his words are immaterial. Salvation is indicated more powerfully by the blue gap in the black clouds through which the light falls across the sails and spume-covered waves. It is not the figure of Christ which is in the foreground. Instead, it is the Christian faith itself which is the target of the depiction.

Revelation also plays an important part in the small-format painting *Christ Showing the Unbelieving Thomas his Wounded Side* (ill. p. 84) from 1634. The scene follows a long tradition. In Chapter 20 of the Gospel according to St John the story is told of how the risen Christ appears to the disciples. Thomas, who was not present, does not believe the others. Eight days later Christ appears to them again, shows them the stigmata and speaks to Thomas, saying,

'Reach hither thy finger, and behold my hands; and reach hither thy hand, and thrust it into my side: and be not faithless, but believing. And Thomas answered and said unto him, My Lord and my God. Jesus saith unto him, Thomas, because thou hast seen me, thou hast believed: blessed are they that have not seen, and yet have believed.'

Since the Middle Ages the admonition of the risen Christ had been equated in art with the question of unbelief. Thomas was always depicted at the moment of placing his hand into Christ's wounded side. In the Bible text on which Rembrandt based his work, the Gospel according to St John, this is not the case. Christ and Thomas are caught in the otherwise dark room in a radiant light which is further strengthened by the reddish aura surrounding Christ's head. Christ is raising his robe - a sort of toga - and pointing to the side wound. Thomas recoils in terror. The hand which he traditionally places in the wound is pressed against his body in a defensive gesture. The disciples and Mary, who is not mentioned in the Bible text, all behave differently. The majority, among them the Virgin Mary, are following events with curiosity. Peter, who is standing nearest to Christ, is bending well forward in order to be able to see the wound clearly. One has got up from his chair in order to be able to see better over the heads of the others. Four have remained modestly in the background. Two of them have their hands folded, but only the disciple pictured on the right is praying. On the right in the foreground lies John, Christ's favourite disciple and the author of the gospel. He appears to be sleeping. Yet this impression is deceptive. John is the great

The Abduction of Ganymede, 1635
Canvas, 171 x 130 cm.
Bredius 471
Dresden, Staatliche Kunstsammlungen, Gemäldegalerie

visionary among the apostles and as such is often depicted sleeping. In this case he is also, as the author of the gospel, the one who does not see and yet believes.

The complexity of the picture is fascinating. In some aspects Rembrandt has adhered to the Bible text. Thomas, for example, does not comply with Christ's instructions to place his hand in the side wound, but says the words, 'My Lord and my God'. In addition, the blessed, those who do not see and yet believe, are represented by the sleeping John. In his depiction of the other disciples, however, Rembrandt does not refer to the Bible text. Here he plays the observer and shows various forms of human behaviour: the inner communion of the man at prayer with his eyes closed, but also the pretence of this in the disciple on the left, who, although he has his hands folded, cannot avert his eyes from the scene. Timidity causes others to remain in the background. The majority, however, openly show their curiosity. Peter's eyes are almost popping out of his head, and the man kneeling on the stairs in the foreground feels the need to comment on everything. The disciples are not depicted as saints who are above human behaviour. Not only Thomas, but also the others, have their faults. By demonstrating their unbelief, sanctimoniousness and curiosity, they become figures with whom the beholder can identify.

Rembrandt again proves his capacity for emotional penetration in the grisaille known as *John the Baptist Preaching* from 1634 (ill. p. 85). This painting in grey and brown tones was supposedly intended as the model for an etching which was never executed. Incorporated into a marvellous landscape stands John the Baptist on a spot surrounded by Roman ruins. The column bearing the head of a Roman emperor towers above him. Many people have gathered to be baptised; some have come from distant lands. They are listening attentively to Christ's harbinger. On the edge of the crowd we see children playing and mothers helping their little ones to relieve themselves. In amongst the listeners two children are having a tussle, and a mother tries to pacify her sobbing child. In the foreground stand three elderly men who are not following the sermon. They are deep in conversation. The picture illustrates Chapter 3 of the Gospel according to St Luke. Many of the details - for example the elderly men, who are identified as Pharisees - can be interpreted iconographically. But alongside them, Rembrandt has also illustrated the types of human behaviour typically seen at mass meetings. This facilitates identification with the biblical figures, which was a major criterion for the faith of the Reformed Church.

In 1640 Rembrandt painted *The Visitation* (ill. p. 86), also known as *The Meeting of Mary and Elizabeth*. Once again he chose a traditional theme and one which had played an important part in Mariological cycles in particular since the Middle Ages. Chapter 1 of the Gospel according to St Luke tells how the pregnant Mary visits her much older cousin Elizabeth, who is approaching her confinement. As the two women greet each other with an embrace Elizabeth's baby, John the Baptist, leaps in his pregnant mother's belly. 'And Elizabeth was filled with the Holy Ghost: And she spake out with a loud voice, and said, Blessed art thou among women, and blessed is the fruit of thy womb.' In the Bible the setting for this event, of this revelation, is given as Elizabeth's house, yet the scene was generally depicted in the open air. Rembrandt too follows this tradition. In the background he places the panorama of a city

Christ in the Storm on the Sea of Genezareth, 1633
Canvas, 160 x 127 cm. Bredius 547
Boston, Isabella Stewart Gardner Museum

82

83

Christ Showing the Unbelieving
Thomas his Wounded Side, 1634
Wood, 53 x 51 cm. Bredius 552
Moscow, Pushkin Museum

John the Baptist Preaching, c. 1635–1636
Canvas on wood, 62 x 80 cm
Bredius 555
Berlin–Dahlem, Staatliche Museen, Gemäldegalerie

in Judaea 'in the hilly country', a city which is not named in the Bible. The backdrop to the actual event is the main entrance to a house whose architecture is reminiscent of that of the ancient world. Since the fifteenth century and in the Netherlands in particular classical architecture had been a symbol of the Old Testament, which had been superseded by the Christian *heilsgeschichte* (redemption through Christ). It is in this way that the entrance must be seen here too. Further references to redemption through Christ include the peacock (the immortality of Christ), the vine tendril (symbol of Christ) and also Joseph (as a representative of the Old Testament) climbing the steps with an ass. In the centre stand the two women, filled with the light of the Holy Ghost. Zacharias, leaning on the shoulder of a boy, steps out of the door. He is no more part of the action than the servant girl and Joseph.

Also painted in 1640 was a small panel depicting *The Holy Family* (ill. p. 88), which for a long time was interpreted as a scene in genre style. The carpenter Joseph is engrossed in his work at the back of the room. Mary is sitting on the floor and nursing her baby, which is brightly lit by the sun as it shines through the window. Next to them Mary's mother Anna has been reading from a book and is now bending over the infant.

This gesture can be seen either as human sentiment or as a moment of revelation.

In his histories from the New Testament Rembrandt displayed a talent for linking redemption through Christ with human sentiments conveying confirmation, revelation or - as in the Passion series - compassion. In this regard he was in step with the conventions of the age. He met the requirements of the Reformed Church. What is interesting is that for all these historical pictures, except the painting of *Peter's Ship*, he chose small formats, which have a more intimate quality than larger-format pictures.

However, when illustrating stories from the Old Testament Rembrandt selected small formats and compositions similar to those used for the aforementioned scenes from the New Testament only when the Old Testament stories concerned did not tell of great heroes but instead invited inner communion. Two excellent examples of this are *The Departure of the Sunamitic Woman*, for a long time interpreted as *The Dismissal of Hagar* (ill. p. 89), and the pictures which recount the story of Tobit (ill. p. 92).[14] *Susannah at the Bath* (ill. p. 90) had occupied a special position in painting since the sixteenth century, for the story of Susannah offered the painter - and thus also Rembrandt - the opportunity to depict a female nude in its erotic dimensions. But most of the paintings which illustrate scenes from the Old Testament are in larger formats than and composed differently from those which depict stories from the New Testament. The explanation for this is to be found in the country's political background.

In the nascent republic of the free Netherlands the Old Testament was not merely of relevance to the Christian faith, it also conveyed political ideas. Out of the war of independence had grown a national consciousness which had to be given substance. The question of a common origin arose. It was found in the tribe of the Batavians, a Germanic people which had lived at the mouth of the Rhine and had been under Roman rule since the first century BC. Furthermore, a parallel was drawn between the republic and the people of Israel. Just as God had led his chosen people out of Egyptian slavery to the Promised Land, so he had now freed the Netherlands from its Spanish yoke. This notion was also established in writing. One example is the 1626 *Nederlandtsche Gedenck-Clanck* (Dutch commemorative anthem) by Adrianus Valerius, in which he describes the oppression of the Dutch by the Spaniards and their liberation. Valerius concludes the text with a prayer in which he focuses upon the comparison between the peoples of Israel and of the free republic,

'... and [you] guided us here in our own interests, just as you led the children of Israel out of Babylonian captivity; parting the waters before us and leading us dry-footed between them, just as the people of Moses and Joshua were brought at that time to the Promised Land ... In your goodness, oh Lord, you have given us many brave men, Jephthah and Samson and many more, to slay the raging lions, dragons and bears which wanted to tear us apart. Yes, nor did the gallant and true David, a shining paragon of piety, fail us; ... In this way ... radiantly were spread your divine word and your truth ... and many people ... led along the correct path and to these beautiful meadows, to this land abounding in water, brimming over with milk and honey, and to the securely walled cities.'[15]

The Meeting of Mary and Elizabeth, 1640
Wood, 56.5 x 47.9 cm. Bredius 562
Detroit, Institute of Arts

The Holy Family, 1640
Wood, 41 x 34 cm. Bredius 563
Paris, Musée du Louvre

Seen from this angle, those of Rembrandt's pictures which are dedicated to this theme can appear in a different light. Explained too are his reasons for preferring powerful large-format paintings to more intimate pictures when depicting the heroes of the Old Testament. Thus *Belshazzar Sees the Writing on the Wall* (ill. p. 94), painted around 1635, can be linked with the war of independence conducted by the Dutch provinces. The story of Belshazzar is told in Chapter 5 of the Book of Daniel. At a great feast the Babylonian king, Belshazzar, sends for the golden vessels which his father, Nebuchadnezzar, had stolen from the temple in Jerusalem. He fills them with wine, drinks from them and thus desecrates them. Soon afterwards a hand appears and writes on the wall something which none of the king's scholars can decipher, whereupon Belshazzar calls for the Jew Daniel, who reads out to him and interprets the words '*mene mene tekel upharsin*'. The words are notification of the fall of Belshazzar's kingdom. The Babylonian king is killed the very same night, and the kingdom of Babylon is lost to Persia. In his rectangular painting Rembrandt hints at the feast with the corner of a table on which stand some of the golden vessels from the temple at Jerusalem. Sitting at the table and staring in horror at Belshazzar, who has leapt out of his seat, are a man and three women. Belshazzar's royalty is clearly indicated by his crown and clothing. His arms are stretched out in horror

'Rembrandt'
The Departure of the Sunamitic Woman, 1640
Wood, 39 x 53 cm. Bredius 508
London, Victoria & Albert Museum

and he has knocked over one of the golden goblets with one hand. As a result of this sweeping movement he takes up a great deal of space in the picture. He is staring at the wall behind him on which the hand, which comes out of a cloud, has just written the last letter. The glowing golden script is surrounded by a bright aura which proclaims the divine nature of the message. The horror is visible not only in the facial expressions of those present, but also in their hands. It is as if they all wished to check this one hand. The warning to the Spaniards that the same would happen to them as happened to the Babylonians if they continued to claim the right to rule the Dutch provinces is clear. The picture is thus a political programme.

Leaving aside the question of content, the picture is also a source of enlightenment about the way in which Rembrandt worked. His methods when appropriating subject matter such as this can be demonstrated with the help of a detail, namely the writing on the wall. Rembrandt paints the Hebrew letters not horizontally from right to left, but vertically. His suggestion that no one other than Daniel could read the script because it was coded by the order of the letters was taken from Rabbi Menasseh

Susannah at the Bath, 1636
Wood, 47.2 x 38.6 cm. Bredius 505
The Hague, Mauritshuis

Susannah at the Bath, 1636
Detail

'Rembrandt'
Tobias Healing his
Father's Blindness, 1636
Wood, 47.2 x 38.8 cm. Bredius 502
Stuttgart, Staatsgalerie

ben Israel (1604-1657). Menasseh was a learned man who at the early age of 18 had written a Hebrew grammar and, because it was not possible to print Hebrew in Amsterdam, had established a printing shop. Here were published not only this grammar, but also further writings of his and of other Jewish authors. Menasseh has gone down in history because of the fact that it was his conversations with the English statesman Oliver Cromwell (1599-1658) in the 1650s which led to the lifting of the ban on Jews entering England - a ban which had been in force since 1290.

Rembrandt and Menasseh were acquainted. After 1639 they were neighbours in *Breestraat*, and Rembrandt did four etchings for the 1655 publication *Piedra gloriosa*. A portrait of the rabbi which Rembrandt etched in 1636, however, proves conclusively that the two men had already known each other for some time. Not until 1639, in his book *De terminu vitae*, did Menasseh associate himself with the idea expounded in the Kabbala that the letters in the Belshazzar story had appeared vertically underneath each other on the wall. Yet Rembrandt had painted his picture earlier than this. His contact with Menasseh must therefore have been so close by the middle of the 1630s that he could ask the rabbi's advice without further ado.

This brief episode demonstrates that it was not only written sources and picture traditions which provided Rembrandt with essential help in

The Angel Leaving
Tobias and his Family, 1637
Wood, 68 x 52 cm. Bredius 503
Paris, Musée du Louvre

מתתוס
נקפי
אלרית

Belshazzar Sees the
Writing on the Wall, *c.* 1635
Canvas, 167.6 x 209.2 cm
Bredius 497
London, National Gallery

shaping his historical paintings, but also his debates with the scribes of his time.

During the next few years Rembrandt painted three incidents from the life of Samson. The Samson theme was one which Rembrandt had already used in his contest with Jan Lievens in Leiden (ill. p. 40). The three paintings from the 1630s are not a cycle. They were painted - not in chronological order - between 1635 and 1638.

The Jew Samson was one of the heroes of the early Israeli period, and his deeds are recorded in the Book of Judges. After the exodus of the children of Israel from Egypt and the seizure of the city of Jericho, the Israelites began to disobey God. As punishment, they were enslaved first by the Midianites and then by the Philistines.
After forty years of slavery God sent the world Samson, who from birth was blessed with a miraculous strength which was vested in his hair. Once grown up, he asked for the hand of the daughter of a Philistine. On the way to court her he encountered a lion and defeated it. As he returned home he found that a swarm of bees had descended upon the body and helped himself to the honey-filled honeycombs. His encounter with the lion was the solution to the puzzle which he set the Philistines at his wedding. 'Out of the eater came forth meat, and out of the strong came forth sweetness.' His bride revealed the solution to her country-

men. On discovering this, Samson slaughtered thirty Philistines in his fury.

Not long afterwards he wanted to visit his wife, but following the unsuccessful wedding her father had given her to another and offered Samson his younger daughter instead. Samson rejected the offer and in anger burnt the Philistines' fields. Their attempts to capture him failed because of his miraculous strength. Not until he fell in love with Delilah did the Philistines succeed in outwitting him. They bribed Delilah and made her promise to discover the secret of his miraculous strength. Pressed by Delilah, Samson revealed to her that his strength would disappear if he were deprived of his hair. Delilah lulled him to sleep, cut off his hair and handed him over to the Philistines, who blinded him and held him captive. It did not occur to them, however, that his strength would return when his hair grew again. Some time later Samson was due to sing at a celebration. Instead he tore the building's supporting columns from their anchorages. The house collapsed over the Philistines' heads and carried them all to their deaths. The moral of the tale is that a hero can defend himself against the treachery and vileness of his enemy only through strength. The loss of this is his downfall.

In 1638 Rembrandt painted *Samson Posing the Riddle to the Wedding Guests* (ill. p. 97). Seated together at a large table are the Philistines with their wives, eating, drinking and joking. This left-hand part of the painting could just as easily be a tavern scene of the kind frequently depicted in the Dutch art of the day. Pushed somewhat to the right of the centre we find the enthroned bride bearing Saskia's features and wrapped in splendid robes. Impassively she looks straight ahead. The carpet behind her, which is intended to distinguish her from the crowd, serves to emphasise the division of the picture. At the front end of the table sits Samson, her husband. He has turned his back to his wife and is already asking the men who encircle him the riddle. Some of them are peering at the woman who will later betray her husband.

By dividing the composition into two Rembrandt succeeds in creating tension. The harmless celebration on the left contrasts with Samson posing the riddle on the right. The two groups are separated by the bride. It is not Samson, but she, who is the main character, and it is her isolation that hints, even at this early stage, at the betrayal.

Rembrandt's painting of the seldom-depicted theme *Samson Threatening his Father-in-law* (ill. p. 96) is powerful indeed. Apart from a black servant, who almost vanishes into the background, only the two adversaries are visible. Samson raises his fist angrily to the old man, who is looking out of the window and making a calming and apologetic gesture. But behind his apparent friendliness there is malice and cunning too. Never before and never again, however, did Rembrandt depict brutality and violence so directly as in the painting *The Blinding of Samson* (ill. p. 98). Samson lies on the ground in a tent, overpowered by the Philistines. Some are dressed in knight's armour and some in oriental robes. They are holding the overpowered Samson firmly, clapping him in chains and threatening him with a lance and a sabre. At the same time one of the Philistines is thrusting a knife into his eye, and Samson's blood is spurting forth. The once-powerful Samson is no longer able to defend himself. His body rears up, but it is no longer an act of strength, merely an expression of pain. Delilah hurries past him to the door of the tent. She has turned to look at him, but shows no remorse for her betrayal of

Samson Threatening
his Father–in–law, c. 1635
Canvas, 158.5 x 130.5 cm
Bredius 499
Berlin–Dahlem, Staatliche Museen,
Gemäldegalerie

him. In one hand she holds her trophy, the magnificent mop of curls, and in the other the weapon, a pair of shears. The figure of Samson symbolises courage, above all through his final act, in which he himself finds death. In *The Blinding of Samson* this courage is trodden underfoot by the Philistines (= Spaniards). But though his betrayal, symbolised in human form by Delilah, can sap Samson's courage, it cannot break it.

Landscapes

Rembrandt painted few landscapes, and in terms of output they represented an insignificant part of his work as a painter (though this was not the case in his graphic work - drawing and etching). In terms of style and composition, however, they were pioneering. Yet as so often happens in the history of art, it was not his contemporaries who recognised this, but painters who lived and worked generations later.

Landscape painting enjoyed great popularity in the Netherlands of the seventeenth century, though no great value was placed upon it by art theoreticians. The trend had begun during the Italian Renaissance when at the end of the sixteenth century painters, particularly in Bologna, started to depict idealised landscapes, and continued into the seventeenth century. The reproduction of paintings in the form of engravings and etchings and more importantly the travels of the artists themselves meant that the

*Samson Posing the Riddle to the
Wedding Guests*, 1638
Canvas, 126 x 175 cm. Bredius 507
Dresden, Staatliche
Kunstsammlungen, Gemäldegalerie

Italians, French, Flemish and Dutch were able to influence each other.
Yet this did not bring about a universal style of landscape painting. The
ideal landscape took different, local, forms.

In the Netherlands of the 1630s depictions of the ideal landscape had
been largely superseded by realistic depictions of landscapes in which the
specialists, that is the painters who specialised in landscape painting,
recorded the vastness of their country, often populated by man and beast.
By the time Rembrandt began to paint, draw and etch landscapes he was
already known far beyond the borders of the republic as a historical
painter and portraitist. In the sphere of graphic art his output also
included realistic reproductions of his surroundings - of Amsterdam and
its environs. As far as painting was concerned, however, he concentrated
on the ideal landscape, despite the fact that it had been recently and generally superseded by the 'landscape portrait'. He seemed to reach back
into the past and in doing so adopted elements of the style of a painter
from the previous generation, Hercules Pietersz. Seghers (1589/90-
1635/39). Seghers clearly was a lasting influence on Rembrandt. The
inventory of Rembrandt's belongings drawn up in 1656 when notice was
given of his insolvency lists no fewer than seven landscape paintings by
Seghers. Whether Rembrandt trained himself directly from these by
making copies of them is not known. But his was indeed a continuation

98

The Blinding of Samson, 1636
Canvas, 236 x 302 cm. Bredius 501
Frankfurt, Städelsches
Kunstinstitut

Landscape with a
Stone Bridge, *c.* 1638
Wood, 29.5 x 42.5 cm. Bredius 440
Amsterdam, Rijksmuseum

of Seghers' work, for just as he first returned to painting historical pictures in Amsterdam when his teacher Lastman was so ill that he could no longer work, so Rembrandt painted his first landscapes only after Seghers' death. Though in his historical paintings Rembrandt had already distanced himself from his teacher's work, at precisely the same time as he did so he took a step 'backwards', so to speak, in respect of his landscape paintings, for they were closely linked to those by Seghers. This also explains why Seghers' late work *The Mountain Landscape*, painted in 1630 and now in the Uffizi in Florence, was until 1871 attributed to Rembrandt. Despite his recourse to the painting style of Seghers, Rembrandt's landscapes are anything but conservative, for stylistically, in terms of their expressiveness, they are way ahead of their time.

Seghers had been endowed with the ability to express certain moods, such as melancholy or loneliness, in his landscapes and consequently he is regarded today as the most progressive landscape painter before Rembrandt and as a forerunner of the Romantic artists. Rembrandt took Seghers' compositions and developed them further. Mountains on which castle ruins tower, stone bridges and, above all, skies dominated by storm-clouds - which plunge the landscape into a sombre mood and cause the sun to cast bright speckles - are the characteristic features of Rembrandt's landscapes. Not only was his use of chiaroscuro superior to that of Seghers, his work was also far more expressive.

Dominating the 1638 painting *Landscape with a Stone Bridge* (ill. p. 100) is the sky with its gathering storm-clouds. The sun rarely punctures the clouds. It bathes a hut and the surrounding trees and bushes in a strange, harsh, almost white light. The river and boats, the field and the distant village are already enveloped in darkness. All that can be seen of the village is the church tower. A similar sombre mood - and one which strikes the beholder as somewhat odd - is also captured in Rembrandt's *Landscape with the Good Samaritan* (ill. p. 101) from the same year. In the foreground stands a large reddish-brown tree, which forms the boundary between a sunken road and the landscape opening out ahead. The landscape is lit by the sun; a yellow cornfield is framed by trees, bushes, windmills and a mountain. On the right-hand side of the picture we see the Good Samaritan, who has placed the man attacked by brigands on his horse and is now heading for the next inn, as reported in the parable from Chapter 10 of the Gospel according to St Luke. The figures on the right may be the priest and the Levite who ignored the unfortunate victim and continued on their way. Under the tree hunters are shooting at birds. They have nothing to do with the central narrative, but merely populate the landscape.

Landscape with the Good Samaritan, 1638
Wood, 46.5 x 66 cm. Bredius 442
Cracow, Czartoryski Muzeum

Stormy Landscape, 1638
Wood, 52 x 72 cm. Bredius 441
Braunschweig, Herzog
Anton–Ulrich–Museum

This barely distinguishable right-hand side of the painting, in which the story takes place, is overshadowed by black storm-clouds. The tree in the centre of the picture stretches like a huge flame into the black sky. Inevitably, one feels forced into a comparison with the cypresses which Vincent van Gogh (1853-1890) was to paint more than two centuries later. Van Gogh was greatly influenced by Rembrandt's painting and copied several of his works. The impression given here, however, is that Rembrandt anticipated a development which was not properly established until the end of the nineteenth century. When viewing a landscape such as this one can appreciate the opinion noted down by a Utrecht lawyer with an understanding of art after a visit to Leiden back in 1628. 'This son of a Leiden miller', he wrote, 'counts for a great deal, but too soon.'[16]

Rembrandt's pictures were thus too modern for his contemporaries. Although his innovations in the fields of portrait painting, historical painting and portraits of the artist brought him success after 1628 and until the classical courtly style became popular around the middle of the century, in his landscapes he obviously went too far for the public. The general trend advanced along other, apparently more objective, paths which led, among other things, to a form of landscape painting which could not have been more true to life. Rembrandt's return to the depiction of ideal landscapes combined with his emotional utterances expressed in terms of stylistic innovation, in expressiveness, were not popular at that time.

Thus he was not granted much success with his landscapes. The aforementioned inventory listed only ten landscape paintings by the artist. He could not have painted many more. Only seven of the paintings known today are still held to be authentic. The rest are thought to have been painted by his pupils.

The teacher and his studio practice

In 1640 Rembrandt was the most successful painter in Amsterdam. It was his pictures which determined the style of the times. He had married a rich woman, bought a house in a genteel street in Amsterdam and now lived side by side with other well-known painters, rich, educated Jews and affluent merchants. The growth in his self-confidence as a result of his success is plain for all to see in his self-portrait (ill. p. 106) from 1640. He depicts himself in aristocratic pose, his arm resting on a balustrade, clad in splendid clothes. This aristocratic picture was modelled on paintings by Titian and Raphael, which at the time were hanging in the house of the Portuguese Jew Alfonso Lopez (1572-1649). Lopez lived alternately in Amsterdam and Paris and he and Rembrandt were in close contact.

River Landscape with Ruins, c. 1650
Wood, 67 x 87.5 cm. Bredius 454
Kassel, Staatliche
Kunstsammlungen

Landscape with a Castle, c. 1640
Wood, 44.5 x 70 cm. Bredius 450
Paris, Musée du Louvre

*Landscape with a Water–
surrounded Castle,* c. 1641
Wood, 45.7 x 63.8 cm. Bredius 451
London, Wallace Collection

Winter Landscape, 1646
Wood, 17 x 23 cm. Bredius 452
Kassel, Staatliche
Kunstsammlungen

*Landscape with
Arched Bridge,* c. 1638
Wood, 28 x 40 cm. Bredius 445
Berlin–Dahlem, Staatliche Museen,
Gemäldegalerie

When Raphael's portrait of Baldassare Castiglione was auctioned in April 1639 and acquired by Lopez, Rembrandt was present and made a sketch of the painting. It was this sketch which formed the basis of his self-portrait. His pupils, however, were not permitted to borrow in this way. They were often required to make copies of his work, but even when the choice of theme was their own his were the only painting techniques whose stylistic and compositional principles they were permitted to borrow.

Since becoming an independent painter Rembrandt had been training pupils. In all, more than fifty pupils and apprentices must have passed through his studio practice. Although this contravened the rules of the Guild of St Luke, which permitted at most three pupils at any one time in one studio, Rembrandt was not alone in circumventing the regulations.

He had begun to take on apprentices back in Leiden. One of his first pupils, Isaac Jouderville (1612/13-1648/53), even accompanied him to Amsterdam. Shortly after Jouderville entered the studio his parents died. The records of the Leiden orphans' court are a priceless source of information regarding the technical side of training with Rembrandt. Even in the early years the master demanded 100 guilders a year for training apprentices; board and lodging was not included. That was a very large sum. Indeed, in Delft 50 guilders was regarded as a lot. Yet throughout his life Rembrandt was able to command this large sum for training pupils. Sandrart says as much in his biography of Rembrandt. He mentions the same sum and adds that the number of genteel children staying at the studio at the same time was nigh on incalculable. The painter's pupils must obviously have had relatively rich parents who could afford to pay the high apprenticeship premium. Jouderville's parents, for example, were the owners of a renowned Leiden guest-house. Their interest in art was great, and they sponsored painters, musicians and poets. Their daughters married painters, their second son became a bookseller. Jouderville had already finished his apprenticeship when he went with Rembrandt to Amsterdam. There he continued to copy his master's paintings and painted others in the master's style which Rembrandt then signed in order that he might sell them at a higher price.

Self–portrait, 1640
Canvas, 102 x 80 cm. Bredius 34
London, National Gallery

Saskia as Flora, 1641
Wood, 98.5 x 82.5 cm. Bredius 108
Dresden, Staatliche
Kunstsammlungen,
Gemäldegalerie

We know that Rembrandt did not use his own art collection for train-ing purposes. His pupils were permitted to copy only his paintings in order that they might adopt his style as their own. He also had them copy the drawings which he did exclusively for teaching purposes.

In Amsterdam Rembrandt was thus not only an established painter, but also a respected teacher. Yet not all of the pupils whom Rembrandt instructed in the art of painting were apprentices. Many a young man from a 'good family' attended the studio for a short time for pleasure without regarding painting as a vocational objective. Others had already concluded their apprenticeships and wanted to learn more from Rembrandt's style of painting, just as Rembrandt had gone to Lastman in Amsterdam after the conclusion of his apprenticeship in order to acquire a more solid grounding.

Another of Rembrandt's pupils was a young man from Cleve called Govert Flinck (1616-1660), who had completed his three-year apprentice-ship in Leeuwarden and then moved to Amsterdam. In his biography of this painter, Arnold Houbraken gives a detailed account of the reasons. He writes,

'But since Rembrandt's style was praised by all at the time, and one's art had to be fashioned after his to find favour in the eyes of the world, Flinck deemed it advisable to study under Rembrandt for one year, ir order to learn his way of handling oils and his style of painting. In a

short time he was able to imitate it so well that various of his works were thought to be original Rembrandts and were sold as such.'[17]

These few sentences contain a host of information about the training offered at Rembrandt's studio. His painting techniques set the trend, and it was expedient for others to be able to employ them. The major objective of a pupil's training was not innovation, that is that the pupils should outgrow the teacher, as the theory of art demanded, but imitation. If the paintings were good enough, if Rembrandt could recognise perfectly his style, his techniques, then he would sign them, thereby passing them off as his own, and sell them at the price which he commanded for his own paintings. In those days such practices were quite usual. Today they are the cause of many a researcher's headaches as experts try to separate the authentic works from those of the pupils (for a detailed examination of this question see Chapter VI).

The difficulties surrounding the question of original and copy are demonstrated very well by one particular example. In Leningrad there is a large-format Rembrandt entitled *The Angel Preventing Abraham from Sacrificing his Son Isaac* (ill. p. 108). It is signed and dated 'Rembrandt f. 1635'. The theme is handled convincingly. Isaac, depicted not as a child but as a youth, lies on a funeral pyre. His father is forcing his son's face to the ground. He wishes to prevent the youth, whose arms are tied, from defending himself and also to spare him the ghastly sight of his father laying hands on him. In the top left-hand corner an angel has appeared from the clouds. With one hand he clutches at Abraham's right hand, which is about to let the knife fall, and with the other he points upwards. All the while he is looking at Isaac. Abraham has turned to the angel and is looking straight into his face. The hands and gazes of Abraham and the angel are the vehicles which enable us to follow the action. Moreover, they link the three protagonists, causing them to form a circle which is completed by the angel looking at the tied and bound offering. Even if one did not know the story of Isaac's sacrifice, one could still interpret the picture correctly. The manner in which Abraham holds the boy's face is not, for instance, marked by brutality, but is protective. It is clear that he is not acting of his own free will. The angel is preventing him from making the gruesome human sacrifice on instructions from above and indicates as much with his hand, which is pointing upwards.

In Munich there is a painting with the same theme. Its dimensions are almost identical. Even the father and son are depicted in the same pose. The angel, however, appears from the clouds not at the side, but behind. He is viewed from below to a greater extent than the first angel, his face is different and he appears to punish rather than to calm. He does not grip Abraham's wrist gently, but clenches it. With his other hand he does not point clearly upwards, but seems instead to be making a menacing gesture. Also, the divine messenger's gaze is fixed upon Abraham, not Isaac. Thus the harmony of the circle is not achieved. In addition, the picture shows the ram which Abraham sacrifices in Isaac's stead. It is visible at the left-hand edge of the picture. Rembrandt typically omitted such details and concentrated entirely on the essential moment in the story's narrative.

This painting, however, bears a unique signature which can be interpreted in a number of ways: '*Rembrandt. verandert. En overgeschildert. 1636*'. The suggested translation, 'Rembrandt. Revised. And painted

The Angel Preventing Abraham from Sacrificing his Son Isaac, 1635 Canvas, 193 x 133 cm. Bredius 498 Leningrad, Hermitage

over. 1636', from which the conclusion has been drawn that the picture was painted by one of Rembrandt's pupils and corrected by the master, was challenged by Haak in 1969. He understands *'overgeschildert'* as 'repainted' and takes the view that this painting too is a Rembrandt. His view is contradicted by the Rembrandt Research Project. On the basis of X-rays which have since been taken, researchers are now of the opinion that it is indeed the work of a pupil, painted in Rembrandt's studio under his supervision, to which he made a few small corrections. The assumption made previously, that the painting is the work of Govert Flinck, is contradicted by the research team, but no certain alternative is offered.

Here then is an example of a piece of work completed by a pupil in the studio at a time when the model was also still there. The pupil adhered fairly closely to his teacher's composition and technique, but did not copy him slavishly. It is this which makes attribution so difficult. Not until he painted the angel, which he did last, did the pupil take liberties and deviate from the original. It may be that it was these deviations which moved Rembrandt to make such an unusual addition to his signature, for this very angel demonstrates a weakness in the picture: it lacks the calming effect of the original - witness the fact that the harmony of the circle is not achieved - and instead demonstrates power. It is the similarities, however, which are of greatest interest. As far as the Isaac-Abraham group is concerned, they are striking. Particularly amazing are details such as the precious knife with which Abraham intends to make the sacrifice and its sheath, which he wears on his belt. They are identical right down to the last detail, as is the position of the open hand and that of the knife as it falls.

Through these two pictures we have evidence of the way in which pupils in Rembrandt's studio worked and how closely they were expected to conform to their teacher's principles. This is one of the reasons why it is so difficult, even today, to identify which paintings were done exclusively by Rembrandt's hand. Whether such identification is actually worth pursuing is, of course, questionable.

Nor did Rembrandt's studio merely produce copies. Another part of the training programme, the drawing of nudes and plaster figures, is reproduced vividly in a drawing by a pupil (ill. p. 112). Several pupils of different ages are sitting in the corner of the studio and drawing a model seated on a podium. On the balustrade above we can also make out the plaster heads which likewise served as models for drawing. The pupils hold their drawing blocks upright before them so that not their heads, but only their eyes, have to move in order to look from the page to the model. In the background stands the master himself, ready to offer support.

For a group of pupils to work together as they are doing in the drawing was somewhat exceptional and only occurred when a nude model was available. We know that before moving into *Breestraat* Rembrandt rented a warehouse as a studio. There he installed partitions so that each of his pupils and apprentices could work undisturbed. He then installed similar partitions in his house. By renting the warehouse, he managed to separate his household and studio in a way which was not usual at that time. This same separation was also expressed in his pictures, especially in those of Saskia and his later companions, whom he never painted in a family picture with himself, but portrayed only as models.

'Rembrandt'
The Sacrifice of Isaac, 1636
Canvas, 195 x 132.3 cm.
Munich, Alte Pinakothek

111

'Rembrandt'
Pupils Drawing in Rembrandt's Studio, 1650–1660
Drawing, 18 x 26.6 cm.
Darmstadt, Hessisches Landesmuseum

In the 1640s Rembrandt's fame began to wane. The baroque style, imported from France and described as the classical courtly style, met with ever greater approval. Unlike many of his pupils, Govert Flinck for example, Rembrandt did not follow the change of style. Yet although he was consequently no longer setting the trend in the Amsterdam art world, he neither lost his reputation as a teacher nor wanted for commissions.

9   According to Schama 1988, p. 651

10 Alpers 1989, p. 134

11 Cit. in Schwartz 1985, p. 110

12 ibid., p. 112

13 ibid., p. 117

14 *The Departure of the Sunamitic Woman* and *Tobias Healing his Father's Blindness* are no longer attributed to Rembrandt himself, but to his studio. See the Rembrandt Research Project, Vol. III, 1989. On the question of attribution, see Chapter VI, p. 190.

15 Cit. in Schama 1988, pp. 118f

16 Cit. in Tümpel 1986, p. 37

17 Cit. in Schwartz 1985, p. 282

Self–portrait, *c.* 1661–1662
Canvas, 114.3 x 95.2 cm
Bredius 52
London, Kenwood House,
The Iveagh Bequest

Group Portrait of the Company of Frans Banning Cocq of the Arquebusiers, 1642
Canvas, 363 x 437 cm. Bredius 410
Amsterdam, Rijksmuseum (on loan from the city of Amsterdam)

Chapter IV
The mature years

Rembrandt had made a name for himself in Amsterdam in a very short space of time and by 1640 he was established as a highly sought after portraitist. The number of his pupils increased and many artists adopted his style, in particular his manner of self-portraiture.

The Night Watch

It was probably in 1640 that Rembrandt received a commission to paint a group portrait of Frans Banning Cocq and his company of *arquebusiers* (ill. p. 114). The painting was completed in 1642, but not until the end of the eighteenth century did it acquire its present title *The Night Watch*. The *arquebusiers* were the newest of the shooting companies; the oldest, the crossbowmen's companies, had existed since the Middle Ages. Later came the archers, then in 1520 the *arquebusiers* or *Kloveniers*. These shooting companies were charged with defending the city in times of emergency, keeping night watch and forming parades on ceremonial occasions. In 1580 they were incorporated into the civil guard, but they retained their old names and club-houses, which were known as *doelen* (practice ranges). The size of the city made the founding of several companies necessary.

During the 1630s a new club-house was built for the *Kloveniers*. The festival hall was to be decorated with six group portraits depicting the individual companies and one depicting the leading members. At the time it was the largest project of its kind ever tackled in the Netherlands. Between 1638 and 1645 seven commissions were awarded to painters well known in Amsterdam. Rembrandt was among them, but so too were his former pupils Govert Flinck and Jacob Backer (1608-1651) as well as the German Joachim von Sandrart. It had already been established which sections of wall were to house which paintings in order that the painters might be informed in minute detail about the space available for and positioning of their work, that is the height at which the paintings would be hung and the way in which they would be lit. The choice of painter was left completely to the individual companies. Rembrandt was to paint the company of Frans Banning Cocq. According to the sources, there were sixteen people willing to pay something in the region of 100 guilders each for inclusion in the picture, with those in prominent positions paying more and those in the background less. In all, the painter received 1,600 guilders. The painting shows several more than the sixteen people who paid, and why there are only eighteen names listed on the scroll over the archway in the background is not known. From the documented testi-

Maria Trip (1619–1683), 1639. Wood, 107 x 82 cm. Bredius 356
Amsterdam, Rijksmuseum (on loan from the Van Weede Family Foundation)

mony of witnesses at the 1659 proceedings relating to Saskia's legacy, on which Rembrandt's son Titus had a claim, we not only know the price of the painting but are also given a clue as to the date of payment and thereby also of the painting's completion (before Saskia's death in June 1642).

Today *The Night Watch* is one of Rembrandt's most famous paintings and also one of the best known of all European paintings. Since the nineteenth century it has been regarded in Holland as a form of national relic. Such veneration has meant not only that whole generations of art theoreticians have put forward a variety of interpretations of the picture, but also that many myths and legends have been spun about it.

According to legend, it was *The Night Watch* which was largely responsible for the tables turning against Rembrandt and his subsequent lack of success. The subjects were allegedly unhappy with the composition of the group portrait, in which they were depicted in action. In short, Rembrandt's contemporaries totally misjudged the picture and the painter, and it was not until the nineteenth century that his skill and more significantly the importance of the picture were fully recognised. By then the painting's veneer had darkened considerably and as a result the picture was regarded as an outstanding example of chiaroscuro painting. It appears to be a nocturnal scene depicting the *arquebusiers* in action, and was once thought to be of a night watch. However, this notion was later dismissed and consideration given to what kind of event might actually have been taking place. What is certain is that the painting depicts either a historical event or a scene from some well-known stage play on a historical theme.

The legend has endured to this very day. The various theories which comprise it continue to appear not only in newspaper articles but also in academic treatises. Yet a reading of contemporary sources reveals that the picture was by no means rejected in all quarters. On the contrary, although critical voices were raised - as they always are when innovations are made - its innovativeness was acknowledged.

In the family album belonging to Frans Banning Cocq, who was largely responsible for commissioning *The Night Watch*, two pages are devoted to the picture. On the right there is a water-colour copy of the

Alijdt Adriaensdr.
(1591–1656), 1639
Wood, 64.7 x 55.3 cm
Bredius 355
Rotterdam, Museum
Boymans–van Beuningen

Nicolaes van Bambeeck
(1596–1661), 1641
Canvas, 105.5 x 48 cm. Bredius 218
Brussels, Musées Royaux des
Beaux–Arts

painting (ill. p. 120) and on the left a text which reads, 'Sketch of the picture in the great room of the Civic Guard House, wherein the young Seigneur of Purmerlandt as Captain gives orders to the Lieutenant, the Seigneur of Vlaerdingen to have his company of citizens march out.'[18]

Had Cocq totally disapproved of the picture he would most probably not have had it copied for the family album.

In 1678, in Chapter I of the fifth book of his *Introduction to the High School of Painting* (cf. Chapter I, p. 15), Samuel van Hoogstraeten, art theoretician and former pupil of Rembrandt, wrote the following illuminating lines about the picture:

'It is not enough for a painter to arrange his likenesses next to each other in rows, as one sees only too often in the club-houses here in Holland. The real masters are capable of ensuring that their work is governed by a single idea ... Rembrandt did this very well - in the view of many, too forcefully - in his piece in Amsterdam's club-house by concerning himself more with the overall conception of that great picture than with the individual portraits with which he was entrusted. And yet this picture, though still open to criticism on this point, will in my opinion outlive all other works of its kind because it is so graphical in its conception, so artistic in its composition and so powerful that one glimpse and many of the other shooting pieces look like playing cards. Though I would have wished him to bring more light into the picture.'[19]

In addition to putting forward the far-sighted view that *The Night Watch* would outlive all other shooting pieces, the text confirms that Rembrandt's overall composition met the requirements of art theoreticians. The majority of art-lovers were clearly able to appreciate the quality of the picture. Hoogstraeten's praise is all the more convincing because at the time when this former pupil of Rembrandt wrote his treatise he actually rejected his teacher's style.

The final critic to whom we shall give a hearing likewise emphasised the enthusiasm of Rembrandt's contemporaries, but was not altogether decided on his own verdict. In his 1686 biography of Rembrandt (cf. Chapter I, p. 18), Filippo Baldinucci wrote:

'He painted a large picture on canvas which is housed in the house of the *Kloveniers* and in which he portrayed a division of the civil guard, an organisation which was well established there. It brought him fame of the kind hardly ever lavished until then upon a painter in that country. The reason for this, more than any other, was that among the figures there is one who in marching has raised a foot and is carrying a lance in his hand which is depicted so superbly foreshortened that the shaft of the weapon appears to the eye as if it had its full extent although no larger than half a foot on the canvas. The rest, however, is so very confused and jumbled that one can barely distinguish one figure from another, although all have been studied closely from the living models. Fortunately for him, however, his contemporaries admired the picture beyond all measure and he received for it a payment of 4,000 golden guilders.'[20]

Despite Baldinucci's error in respect of the price, it is likely that his utterances on the subject of the enthusiasm which the picture engendered are correct, since he quotes as the source of his information on Rembrandt the artist's pupil Bernhardt Keil (born 1624), who worked in Rembrandt's studio from 1642 until 1644 and thus must have witnessed the completion and reception of *The Night Watch*.

Agatha Bas (1611–1658), 1641
Canvas, 105.2 x 83.9 cm
Bredius 360
London, Buckingham Palace,
Royal Collection

From the family album of Frans Banning Cocq with a copy of The Night Watch, c. 1650
Water–colour, 14.2 x 18 cm
Amsterdam, Rijksmuseum

Govert Flinck (1615–1660)
The Amsterdam Civic Guard Celebrating the Signing of the Peace of Münster, 1648
Canvas, detail
Amsterdam, Rijksmuseum (on loan from the city of Amsterdam)

Though sources covering the execution of *The Night Watch* are excellent, the picture's meaning can only be determined by making some assumptions. Since the second decade of this century researchers have been divided into two camps: those searching for an actual event - for example the reception of Maria de Medici in Amsterdam in 1638 - which could have served as a model, and those who consider that the picture is more likely to be a symbolic representation. On account of the most recent research the Rembrandt Research Project has now come to the conclusion that *The Night Watch* is a 'role portrait' with allegorical allusions. This interpretation has been incorporated into the following description of the picture.

In 1715 the painting, which today measures 363 x 438 cm, was transferred from the *Kloveniersdoelen* to the Small War Council Room in the town hall. At this point it was trimmed down. It is assumed that the original measurements were 393 x 515 cm. The water-colour from Frans Banning Cocq's family album shows in particular more figures on the left. The reduction has clearly detracted from the overall impression given by the painting, especially since it has meant that the ratio of height to width has altered.

The *arquebusiers* have gathered before a large archway, but no military order is identifiable. In the foreground, pushed rather too near to the edge of the picture as a result of the cutting, stands Frans Banning Cocq in the central position. His clothes and his command staff mark him out as the captain. As the text in his family album reveals, he is in the process of issuing to his lieutenant, Willem van Ruytenburgh, the order for the *arquebusiers* to fall into marching formation. The lieutenant too is clothed in accordance with his rank and holds a lance with a decorated blade in his hand.

The way in which these two protagonists are dressed does not merely mark them out as the holders of the highest rank in the company, but is also symbolic. Cocq is clad in the colours of Amsterdam, black and red. The shadow of his hand, which he has stretched out for the purpose of lending urgency to his order, falls across the embroidered border of the lieutenant's jacket at precisely the spot where the Amsterdam coat of arms, three St Andrew's crosses arranged one above the other, is held by a lion. The lieutenant's yellow and white clothing is interwoven with the colour blue as if with delicate threads, although this can only be discerned on the original. Blue and yellow were the colours of the *Kloveniers*. In their central position the two main characters thus represent both the city and its companies of *arquebusiers*. They are both main characters and symbolic figures.

Next to them in the background the *Kloveniers'* weapon, the arquebus, is presented to us by three people. The man dressed in red to the left of Cocq is loading his weapon with gunpowder. Next to him, half obscured by the captain, the soldier dressed in sixteenth-century armour discharges his weapon. On his helmet we can make out fresh oak leaves, the symbol of civic virtue and strength. This symbol was also to be found, worked in silver, on the *Kloveniers'* chain of office. The man in red behind the lieutenant is blowing away the gunpowder remaining after a shot from his arquebus. The use of the weapon is thus demonstrated by three people who are so much a part of the action that their symbolic value becomes apparent only upon closer inspection. Not only the manner in which these figures are depicted and their activities but also the other *arquebusiers* were borrowed relatively unchanged from the *Manual of Arms* written in 1608 by Jakob II de Gheyn (1565-1629), in which the individual grips used in shooting are demonstrated over more than 120 pages.

A central role is played by the sumptuously dressed young girl (a second girl behind her is barely visible) who on the face of it appears to be a sutler, one of those who generally provided the *Kloveniers* with food and drink. Her golden yellow clothing, decorated with blue threads, refers back once again to the *Kloveniers*. In her belt the girl is carrying a fowl whose claws, the *arquebusiers'* heraldic symbol, can be seen with particular clarity. In addition, she holds the guild's drinking horn in her hands. Hence she is a personification of the *Kloveniers*, their symbol and emblem-bearer.

The actions of almost every figure in the painting allude by way of their symbolic content to the city and the company. The lance-bearers on the right are holding their weapons in such a way as to form a St Andrew's cross, Amsterdam's coat of arms. The men appear to be sorting themselves out in readiness for the march. As yet the group is not in place, but is on the point of falling into line. Even the drummer, whom Rembrandt placed in the picture without his having paid for his portrait to be painted, is already present. The painting has other themes too: it expresses the men's pride at serving in the colours of Amsterdam and illustrates the way in which firearms should be handled.

Just as in his first group portrait, *The Anatomy Lecture of Dr Nicolaes Tulp* (ill. p. 50), Rembrandt emphasised the scientific importance of the surgeon, in *The Night Watch* he indicates the significance of the *arquebusiers* by depicting three of them using their weapons. Realistically, target practice would certainly not have taken place before marching off, especially not in so confined a space. Yet this would have been easily decoded by Rembrandt's contemporaries as giving symbolic meaning to the picture. Thus it was not, quite rightly, merely the picture's compositional structure - which depicts the individual figures in action - which was praised. Inspired by Rembrandt, some of the painters who received commissions for the other paintings for the *Kloveniersdoelen* also attempted to liven up their paintings with a little action. They did not succeed as convincingly as Rembrandt did with *The Night Watch* and were unable to endow their pictures so unobtrusively with symbols.

Saskia's death

Saskia died shortly after the completion of *The Night Watch*. Between 1636 and 1640 she had been pregnant three times, yet none of the children had lived more than a few weeks. Three months after the birth of her last daughter she was pregnant again. During this pregnancy she lost her sister Titia, to whom she had been very close. When, in September 1641, she gave birth to a son, he was christened Titus and Titia's husband was asked to be his godfather.

Saskia never recovered from this confinement. She ailed all winter. On 5 June 1642 she made her will in the presence of a notary. Titus was made sole heir, Rembrandt became usufructuary and administrator of the fortune until his death or remarriage. In this eventuality he undertook to repay to Saskia's relatives half of the capital which she had brought into the marriage. Saskia also appointed Rembrandt as the child's guardian,

'Rembrandt'
Self–portrait, c. 1643–1645
Wood, 69 x 56 cm. Bredius 38
Karlsruhe, Staatliche Kunsthalle

thus eliminating any possibility of his ending up in the orphanage. Upon Rembrandt's subsequent insolvency this proved a great misfortune, since after Saskia's death no inventory was compiled of Titus' possessions and these were released for auction along with Rembrandt's. One week after making her will Saskia died, leaving Rembrandt to care for the 9-month-old Titus alone. He engaged a nanny, Geertghe Dircx, the widow of a ship's trumpeter, who was only a few years younger than himself. She and Rembrandt lived together until 1649. Then her place was taken by the 22-year-old Hendrickje Stoffels.

Rembrandt's separation from Geertghe Dircx does not reveal a positive picture of the artist. The only reason that biographers have pounced enthusiastically upon the story is that the historical sources contain eloquent testimony on the subject and reveal the artist's negative behaviour. Once Rembrandt had separated from Geertghe Dircx the courts awarded her alimony, but on the condition that she was not allowed to change her will, in which she cited Titus as her heir, or dispose of any of Rembrandt's gifts to her, including Saskia's jewellery. When, in spite of this, she sold a ring Rembrandt had her imprisoned. He even paid the transport costs. The court's files naturally divulge nothing about their dealings with each other, but even if it was the case that Rembrandt did not know how to free himself of a woman who had become disagreeable to him other than by having her imprisoned, it seems unreasonable to conclude from this that he was of bad character.

During the years which followed Saskia's death Rembrandt's work came to a virtual standstill. There are many theories as to why this happened, of which a few can be refuted. The assumption that he ceased to receive portrait commissions on account of *The Night Watch*, felt by some critics to have been a failure, is no longer seriously supported. Whether Saskia's death affected him so deeply that his capacity for work waned must remain an open question; too little is known of his relationship with his wife. Equally hypothetical is the assumption that as a young widower Rembrandt identified so strongly with his role as a father that he had little time for painting. The drawings of children that he did from 1634 have been interpreted in a recent study as an expression of the artist's desire for children, a desire which was satisfied only with the birth of Titus. Yet Rembrandt continued to dedicate himself to the depiction of children until around 1662, by which time he had already also had a daughter by Hendrickje for more than eight years. Neither is the fact that approximately two years after Saskia's death he drew a man feeding an infant when Titus was probably already able to use a spoon proof of a particularly strong identification with his role as a father. The suggestion that Rembrandt, as a young widower, became totally involved in fatherhood and therefore neglected his painting, seems to me to be too modern an idea.

The reason for the stagnation in Rembrandt's work is much more likely to be found in the stylistic changes taking place in painting at that time and in the artist's mental development. With *The Blinding of Samson* (ill. p. 98), his *Self-portrait* of 1640 (ill. p. 106) and *The Night Watch* (ill. p. 114), he had reached the point at which he needed to examine his own development. As I have already said, the stylistic development of the time was also a factor. The influence of Caravaggio had dwindled. Its place had been taken by a classical-courtly style which later evolved into Rococo. Clear colours and bold contours were the

Christ and the Adulteress, 1644. Wood, 83.8 x 65.4 cm. Bredius 566
London, National Gallery

order of the day. Rembrandt needed to get straight in his own mind whether he wanted to take this course and follow the fashion.

After some fifteen years of continual development which had begun in Leiden and during which he had purposefully pursued his chosen course, he now arrived at a point where he had either to discontinue his previous work and adopt totally new goals and/or at least modify the ideas which he had previously supported. This moment comes in the life of many distinguished artists. Initially Rembrandt's search was expressed in the form of stagnation. Most of the few works which he produced during the period between 1643 and 1650 have since been attributed to his studio. This is true, for example, of the *Self-portrait* dated around 1645 (ill. p. 123). Originally oval, it was expanded - not very carefully - in the eighteenth century to form a rectangle. Painted five years after the aristocratic self-portrait (ill. p. 106), it shows an entirely different Rembrandt. The expensive clothing is no longer quite new and as his gaze settles on the beholder his face is questioning and searching, not self-confident. Since it is probably a studio painting, it is safe to assume that the master approved of such a likeness. He himself returned to his origins. In 1644 he painted the picture *Christ and the Adulteress* (ill. p. 124), a small upright rectangular panel. The scene is set inside the temple in Jerusalem. In the background the altar and high priest are framed by magnificent architecture; in the foreground beneath the altar region stands a group of people gathered around Jesus and the adulteress. Everyone is waiting anxiously to see whether Jesus will absolve the woman of her sins and thus offend against Mosaic law. The Pharisees would then finally have had a reason to apprehend him.

In terms of its composition the picture is very similar to *Simeon in the Temple* (ill. p. 37) of 1631. Even details such as the structure of the temple look the same. Of course, we can also see the way in which Rembrandt had developed over the years. Not only his management of light and his use of chiaroscuro, but also the whole structure of the painting from 1644 exhibit an assuredness which was still lacking in 1631. It is nevertheless remarkable to see how Rembrandt harks back in this painting to his early days as a freelance painter. It is almost as if he wished to start again where he had begun in order to take a different, if not altogether new, path. The repercussions of this retrospection are clearly visible in the few pictures which he painted over the next few years.

The biblical histories of the 1640s

During the 1640s Rembrandt became a Nonconformist. Today he is rightly described as the 'first heretic of painting, who alone has dared to break away from the classicistic rules and seek his own path'.[21] Allowing for the addition of a few principles which he first adopted in Amsterdam, the style of the pictures which he painted in his early Leiden period went unchanged. To all intents and purposes he remained a chiaroscurist. His pictures, however, lost the power which they had radiated in the mid-1630s in particular. They became more intimate and private and emphasised more strongly the question of revelation, which played an important part in the biblical story of the New Testament according to the Calvinist interpretation. A tendency for the content to appear like an extract from a wider scene and theatrical considerations now defined his pictures completely.

The Holy Family with Painted
Frame and Curtain, 1646
Wood, 46.5 x 68.8 cm. Bredius 572
Kassel, Staatliche
Kunstsammlungen

In the mid-1640s scenes from the childhood of Jesus predominated. Particularly remarkable is a painting of the Holy Family (ill. p. 126). This small rectangular panel is enclosed in a painted frame which is rounded off at the top. In front of this is a painted curtain rail complete with red curtain. The curtain is drawn back and screens off part of the right-hand side of the picture. On the left sits Mary in front of the fire. She has taken her child out of its cradle and is pressing it tenderly against her. On the right in the background we can make out the blurred outlines of Joseph, the carpenter, at work. Like *The Night Watch*, the picture has several levels of meaning. The first is Mary's revelation that in her son God has become a man, as represented by the Mother of God illuminated in a room whose architecture reminds us of a church. Mother and child symbolise the New Testament. Joseph is to be found a few steps further back. The wooden ceiling of this part of the room has been destroyed, no light penetrates that far. The curtain in the foreground alludes to that in the temple in Jerusalem, which tore down the middle at the very moment when Christ died the Saviour's death. In the picture it and Joseph represent the Old Testament. But it also has another meaning. Together with the painted frame and the rail it illustrates the now profaned nature of the devotional image of the future, a collector's item whose place will be in a cabinet.

By creating these different levels of meaning Rembrandt was returning to the practice of 'concealing' symbols (disguised symbolism) employed by the early Dutch artists grouped around Jan van Eyck (c. 1390-1441) and Roger van der Weyden (1399-1464) and still in common use in the

The Holy Family with Angels, 1645
Canvas, 117 x 91 cm. Bredius 570
Leningrad, Hermitage

Joseph's Dream in the Stable at Bethlehem, 1645
Wood, 20 x 27 cm. Bredius 569
Berlin–Dahlem, Staatliche Museen, Gemäldegalerie

sixteenth century. The painters of the fifteenth century had used scenes depicting the Virgin Mary in particular as a pretext for painting furnished living rooms and incorporating symbols of the Virgin and prefigurations in these interiors. Rembrandt would not have needed to tread this path. In order to depict man in his living space he would merely have had to concentrate on another subject: the scene in genre style. For Rembrandt's contemporaries the fact that he nevertheless furnished the rooms in which we see Mary with her child (ill. p. 126) or Tobit with his wife (ill. p. 129) with a variety of details intended to give the idea of a modest household and a carpenter's workshop suggested the possibility of identification. The painting's symbols, which are recognisable only with difficulty and which refer to certain places in the Bible, are often the only clue to the fact that the scene is a biblical one. Yet what is actually new about the pictures is not their content, but their style. As he had done previously, Rembrandt distinguished and differentiated his compositions according to theme. Particularly remarkable in this respect are two small panels known as *Joseph's Dream in the Stable at Bethlehem* (ill. p. 128) and *Abraham Serving the Three Angels* (ill. p. 129). *The Adoration of the Shepherds* (ill. p. 131) belongs to the same group.

Tobit with his Wife Anna, 1645
Wood, 20 x 27 cm
Bredius 514
Berlin–Dahlem,
Staatliche Museen,
Gemäldegalerie

Abraham Serving the Three Angels,
1646
Wood, 16 x 21 cm
Bredius 515
Aurora Trust

'Rembrandt'
*The Adoration
of the Shepherds*, 1646
Canvas, 65.5 x 55 cm. Bredius 575
London, National Gallery

Common to these pictures is a very hazy style of painting. Neither the bodies nor the faces of the figures are elaborated. Rembrandt sets more store on the overall composition than on the details. He does, on the other hand, attach great importance to the depth of the rooms (or landscapes) and the interaction between the figures. The light does not shine on a figure or group, but from a figure in order to indicate his or her divinity. This is at its clearest in *The Adoration of the Shepherds*. The light radiates from the infant Jesus, who is reposing, barely discernible, on the straw. It is shining so brightly and brilliantly that the faces of all those around him also gleam. It is also reflected in the faces of the shepherds, who have not yet penetrated as far as the child.

This Adoration is interesting for another reason too. In the same year as it was painted, 1646, Rembrandt also completed a very much smaller painting on the same theme which mirrors its composition exactly. Though both dated and signed, it has recently been attributed to a pupil of Rembrandt. The accuracy of this attribution, which originates with Tümpel, could well be decided by the Rembrandt Research Project, but Rembrandt must also have acknowledged the picture as the (possible) work of a pupil, otherwise he would not have signed it (cf. Chapter VI, p. 190).

The introspection which Rembrandt now took as the basis of his pictures is illustrated in the two Emmaus pictures of 1648. The wooden

The Adoration of the Shepherds, 1646
Canvas, 97 x 71.3 cm. Bredius 574
Munich, Alte Pinakothek

The Risen Christ at Emmaus, 1648
Wood, 68 x 65 cm. Bredius 578
Paris, Musée du Louvre

panel (ill. p. 132) has remained relatively light. Christ and the disciples are seated at a table in an ill-defined room. The landlord is just bringing the meal. Christ is sitting on a throne-like chair and with its white cloth the table reminds us of an altar. An aura surrounding Christ's head is like a halo. The light which illuminates the entire room emanates from him. Behind him the wall opens up into a niche which is reminiscent of the apse of a church. Christ is looking upwards as he holds the bread in his hands and breaks it. The recognition and alarm indicated by the disciples' gestures are very restrained.

A comparison with the Emmaus picture of 1629 (ill. p. 29) reveals the development which Rembrandt had undergone since then. In the earlier work the Son of God is lit up. This is so potent that the disciples fall to the ground full of terror. The scene demonstrates divine power. In the picture of 1648, on the other hand, Christ is himself the light which shines. Faith and piety are emphasised. In no way is this scene powerful.

A second version of this picture (ill. p. 133) was painted in the same year. To this very day researchers cannot agree whether this painting is the work of pupils or of Rembrandt himself. Many aspects of the wooden panel's composition have been borrowed. The arrangement of Christ and the disciples around the table and their poses are identical. The disciple on the right, however, is turned more towards Christ and the landlord has been joined by a landlady, who is bringing the glasses. Remarkably, it is these two, who do not appreciate the significance of what is happening, who are emphasised most strongly by the light, the source of which remains concealed. Christ and the disciples are more heavily shadowed, with the result that the beholder of the picture cannot follow the gaze of the Son of God. In front of the scene hangs a curtain on a rail.

It is amazing how much a picture changes merely as a result of the way in which light is deployed. In this picture the landlord and landlady are emphasised and the actual protagonists reduced to marginal characters, despite being placed at the centre of the painting. This aspect if nothing else suggests the correctness of the theory that the piece was painted by a pupil, for it is not typical of Rembrandt. That same assessment is very much less plausible in the case of the painting *David's Farewell to Jonathan* (ill. p. 135). The picture was painted back in 1642 and has been interpreted in many ways. It has been regarded, for instance, as *The Return of the Prodigal Son*, *The Reconciliation of Jacob and Esau*, *The Reconciliation of David and Absalom* and just recently as *The Reconciliation of David and Mephiboseth*. The Rembrandt Research Project has decided in favour of *David's Farewell to Jonathan*, for which there are the most points of reference in the picture, but has also, as I have said, designated the painting as the work of a pupil. However the question is resolved, the fact remains that the manner in which this painting expresses human emotion is quite astonishing. An older, richly-clad

'Rembrandt'
The Risen Christ at Emmaus, 1648
Canvas, 89.5 x 111.5 cm
Bredius 579
Copenhagen, Statens
Museum for Kunst

The Rest on the
Flight into Egypt, 1647
Wood, 34 x 48 cm. Bredius 576
Dublin, National Gallery of
Ireland

man clasps in his arms an equally expensively dressed young man. The younger man is pressing his head against the breast of the older man. Over the town in the background clouds are gathering - a sinister omen. The two protagonists in their golden clothing interwoven with precious stones are clearly defined against the background. The boy's blond locks match his robe. The feelings of grief, of sadness at parting and of danger but also of friendship which the two men have are rendered to perfection in this picture. The ability to represent emotions for which Huygens commended the young Rembrandt (cf. Chapter II, p. 40) had since been further developed by the artist in the most astonishing way. It is immaterial to the interpretation of this picture which story is being narrated and which of the aforementioned titles is the correct one; the painting's human dimension does not alter.

A still greater disengagement from its scenic context is displayed by the painting of a young woman in bed, which is generally referred to as *Sarah Waiting for Tobias* (ill. p. 136). The date is disputed. It is commonly assumed that the young woman is Geertghe Dircx, in which case Gary Schwartz's assumption that the piece dates from 1647 may well be accurate.

The story told by this picture is that of Sarah, who is possessed by an evil spirit which has already slain seven men on her wedding night. Tobias has been advised by the angel accompanying him that he should place pieces of the liver and the heart of a fish on the coals before consummating the marriage. In this way he would be able to banish the demon. The identification of the young woman with Sarah is convincing

'Rembrandt', *David's Farewell to Jonathan*, 1642
Wood, 73 x 61.5 cm. Bredius 511. Leningrad, Hermitage

Sarah Waiting for Tobias, 1647. Canvas, 81.3 x 68 cm. Bredius 110
Edinburgh, National Gallery of Scotland

Susannah Surprised by the Elders, 1647. Wood, 76 x 91 cm. Bredius 516 Berlin–Dahlem, Staatliche Museen, Gemäldegalerie

Jean–Etienne Liotard (1702–1790)
*François Tronchin
(1704–1798),* 1757
Pastel on parchment, 38.1 x 46.3 cm. Cleveland, The Cleveland Museum of Art

if one bears in mind that Pieter Lastman painted a picture on the same theme in 1611 in which Sarah is depicted similarly and that in the 1640s Rembrandt's work bore close relation in terms of the choice of theme to the work of his former teacher, although he altered the scenes by singling out a particular moment in the action.

The painting shows a section of the bed. Sarah has partly raised herself up. With one hand she holds back the curtain in order that she can see better. Expectantly and curiously she looks into the - undepicted - room. She is not, however, looking out of the picture, but has fixed her gaze on a point which cannot be seen by the beholder.

Today the painting is of interest in another respect too; it is copied in another picture. In 1757 François Tronchin (1704-1798) had himself painted by Jean-Etienne Liotard (1702-1790) with this picture, which was at that time in his possession. At a time when Rembrandt had not yet regained the recognition which would be his once more in the nineteenth century, an art collector proudly had his portrait painted with this picture. Even then there were admirers of Rembrandt who did not yield to contemporary criticism.

It would be fair to say of Rembrandt's few histories of the 1640s as a whole that they emphasised individuality more strongly than his earlier works. Indeed, the historical paintings of the 1630s, in which Rembrandt depicted scenes from the Old Testament, also had a political dimension.

Girl Leaning on
a Window-sill, 1645
Canvas, 81.6 x 66 cm. Bredius 368
London, Dulwich College Gallery

A Young Jew, *c.* 1648
Wood, 25.1 x 21.5 cm. Bredius 250
Berlin–Dahlem, Staatliche Museen,
Gemäldegalerie

Girl at the Window, 1651
Canvas, 78 x 63 cm. Bredius 377
Stockholm, Nationalmuseum

In them he depicted the Israelite heroes who were regarded during the war of independence as figures with whom the Dutch could identify. During the 1640s, however, Rembrandt painted no more heroes. He selected scenes in which he could express human emotions such as grief, friendship and also curiosity. The scenes themselves, the stories which centred around them, were merely foils against which to depict human behaviour. This was an element which although it had earlier played a part in his pictures now took precedence once and for all over other considerations. The way in which his work developed during the later stages of his life shows that he was seeking to perfect this idea.

Portraits and studies of heads

During the 1630s Rembrandt set great store on pomp and on masquerade. He painted himself and Saskia in various roles and even his studies of heads revealed an enthusiasm for the exotic above all else. Dressed in oriental robes, he could decorate his studies for portraits in all sorts of ways. Yet just as he dispensed in his historical paintings from the 1640s with the demonstration of power, which often included pomp, he now turned to studies of other subjects. In 1645 he painted the picture of a simple young girl leaning on a window-sill and looking out of the window, that

'Rembrandt'
*Young Woman at
a Half–door*, 1645
Canvas, 102 x 84 cm.
Chicago, Art Institute,
Mr and Mrs W. Kimball
Collection

is out of the picture (ill. p. 138). There are no grandiose gestures or expensive clothes. The background comprises a weathered wall of a house criss-crossed by cracks next to the window-sill. The young woman wears a simple white blouse, is propped up on her elbows and has fixed her dark eyes upon the beholder. It is difficult to resist this steady but nevertheless questioning gaze.

Here Rembrandt is no longer describing his subject's character with the aid of externals, but exclusively through the expression on her face and in her eyes. The same can be seen in the portrait of *A Young Jew* (ill. p. 139) from 1648. The face is not as sharply elaborated here as in the picture of the young girl. The brush strokes are more clearly visible in the face. It is a hasty sketch in oil. Yet here too Rembrandt succeeds in capturing the subject's character traits. The soft sensitive mouth complements the eyes, which likewise rest directly on the beholder. The gaze is vague but nevertheless steady.

This tendency towards a psychologising manner of depiction continued over the next few years. In 1651 Rembrandt painted a *Girl Leaning on a Window-sill* (ill. p. 140), which bears a very great similarity to the likeness of a girl painted in 1645, not only physiognomically, but also in terms of the way in which the girls are depicted.

If one compares the picture of a *Young Woman at a Half-door* (ill. p. 141) with these three pictures, one can appreciate the doubts which researchers have raised in recent years as to its authenticity. The pupil of Rembrandt to whom its execution was entrusted must be credited with a great deal of technical skill. Yet he lacked the ability to represent a person's soul. The even application of colour suggests perfectly regular features; there is nothing natural about the figure's pose. This is not a person but an ideal. Gerson has described the figure as 'stiff and lacking in emotion'.[22] The woman is not a living being; she resembles a doll, a wax figure. This impression is strengthened further by the eyes, which neither look out of the picture nor are fixed on another point. The naturalness of movement which had become so characteristic of Rembrandt is lacking.

A study of Rembrandt's portraits reveals a change similar to that

Jan Six (1618–1700), 1654
Canvas, 112 x 102 cm. Bredius 276
Amsterdam, Six Collection

Jan Six (1618–1700), 1647
Etching, fourth state, 24.4 x 19.1 cm
Bartsch 285
Amsterdam, Rijksprentenkabinet

An Old Woman Reading, 1655
Canvas, 80 x 66 cm. Bredius 385
Drumlanrig Castle, Scotland,
collection of the Duke of
Buccleuch

which took place in his studies of heads. It is interesting to note that for some ten years Rembrandt did not execute a single portrait commission. Whether he did not receive any or whether he refused them all is unknown. The theory that he no longer enjoyed recognition after *The Night Watch* and therefore lacked commissions altogether has already been refuted. Even without portrait commissions his earnings were still apparently sufficient and he continued to head a large studio, that is he still had income from his apprentices. Moreover, his reputation as an etcher had now spread far beyond the borders of Holland.

In 1654 Rembrandt painted a portrait of his friend Jan Six (ill. p. 142), whom he had portrayed in an etching back in 1647 (ill. p. 142). Both the etching and the painting are among his most famous works from this period. Jan Six (1618-1700) was a merchant who had also distinguished himself as a playwright and promoter of the arts. Later he became burgomaster of Amsterdam. Rembrandt and he must have met in the mid-1640s. In 1647 Rembrandt completed the etching; in 1648 he was responsible for the frontispiece for the play *Medea*, written by Jan Six and directed by the poet Jan Vos (1610-1667), who for twenty years was the head of the Amsterdam Theatre. In 1653 Jan Six bought three of Rembrandt's paintings from the 1630s. One of these was the portrait of Saskia (ill. p. 57) which shows her as an elegant lady. In the same year Rembrandt borrowed 1,000 guilders from Six, who let him have the loan free of interest. A year later he painted the portrait. Whether it was the portrait or the financial transactions which tipped the scales is not known, but Six turned his back on Rembrandt and in 1656 had a portrait of his intended painted by Govert Flinck. In addition, he also disposed of claims against the painter. Rembrandt's portrait shows the elegantly dressed Jan Six as an impatient man. Svetlana Alpers' interpretation of

Man in a Fur–lined Coat, 1654
Canvas, 114.3 x 87 cm. Bredius 278
Toledo, Museum of Art, Clarence Brown Fund

Nicolaes Bruyningh
(1629/30–1680), 1652
Canvas, 107.5 x 91.5 cm
Bredius 268
Kassel, Staatliche
Kunstsammlungen

the picture points out the artist's competence in taking account of this feature:

'Six is turning slightly. He has thrown his coat over one shoulder and is on the point ... of wanting to leave. Let us just assume that he was not prepared to find the time to sit for Rembrandt. The slight inclination of his head to the side and front and the shadowed eyes could of course signify withdrawal and reticence. Since the location is Rembrandt's studio, however, I think that they are instead characteristic of a model who was resisting the role assigned to him or refusing to submit to the demands which Rembrandt used to make on his models. Six was refusing to conform to the picture of him which Rembrandt was painting. The speed with which the painting was executed and the keenness to leave apparently displayed by the subject, who has not even taken off his outdoor clothes, point to Six as someone breaking free of Rembrandt's spell ... It was these very signs of stubbornness that helped Rembrandt to preserve his picture by adapting his approach in a quite remarkable manner to Six's behaviour.'[23]

18 Cit. in *Rembrandt Research Project* Vol. III 1989, p. 480 (also in *The Age of Rembrandt and Vermeer* by Nash 1972)

19 Cit. in Tümpel 1986, p. 225

20 Cit. in Goldscheider 1960, p. 13

21 Cit. in Tümpel 1986, p. 371

22 Cit. in Tümpel 1986, p. 426

23 Alpers 1989, p. 203

Chapter V
Loss of independence: final works

The final thirteen years of Rembrandt's life have more often than not been described in biographies as the artist's most impoverished. Rembrandt is said to have lived in poverty, abandoned by all, his painting the only thing which kept him alive. In recent years this picture, which was not only painted by Rembrandt himself but is also frequently found in biographical works on the artist, has been revised. Documents published long ago confirm that although in the 1650s Rembrandt no longer enjoyed the full recognition of the Amsterdam art world, as he had done in the 1630s, he was nevertheless well able to maintain his position among the producers of art. Though he no longer possessed riches, he was not short of money. It was during these years, as a mature man, that he painted his most beautiful pictures.

Self-portrait, c. 1655
Wood, 49.2 x 41 cm. Bredius 49
Vienna, Kunsthistorisches
Museum

Insolvency

In 1656, on account of his personal financial position and that of his business, Rembrandt filed a petition for insolvency. The very fact that he did this without having been directly compelled to do so has been ignored by many biographers. Moreover, his dealings with money as a whole have been interpreted very differently, even though the same sources of information were available to the authors responsible. At the beginning of this century, for example, Richard Hamann wrote:

'with the nonchalance of a genial, impractical disposition he squandered and freely distributed money when it would have been better to exchange something of value to him ... The actual reason for his financial ruin lay in the house purchase of 1639, which was forced upon him by his desire for something of his own and for privacy. With the help of his backers and burgomaster Six he was able to stave off total bankruptcy for a while. In 1656 Rembrandt's house, and all his belongings, including his very distinguished collections, went under the hammer.'[24] The word now was that he was down-at-heel and alone. Only three things were important to him: his art, his son and his sweetheart.

Gary Schwartz assesses Rembrandt's financial position very much more realistically, but exaggerates when he says, 'On January 8, 1653, the

Titus Writing, 1655
Canvas, 77 x 63 cm. Bredius 120
Rotterdam, Museum
Boymans–van Beuningen

Hendrickje as Flora, c. 1654
Canvas, 100 x 91.8 cm. Bredius 114
New York, Metropolitan Museum
of Art, gift from Archer M.
Huntington in memory of Collis
Potter Huntington

financial side of Rembrandt's life turned sour, bringing complications that were to plague him and others for the rest of his life'.[25] Rembrandt himself does not seem to have suffered a great deal from the circumstances which he had created.

Accordingly, Svetlana Alpers too sees in him a market-orientated artist, who was looking to find 'a niche for his art in the developing capitalist market system'.[26] She describes Rembrandt's practice of incurring debts and offering as security paintings which were not yet finished as that of running a business which relied on the willingness of his customers and creditors to speculate: 'Instead of conscientiousness or a feeling of obligation it was monetary and market economy considerations which were behind his dealings with buyers and customers. Rembrandt clearly felt better if he could bring his paintings into circulation through transactions with his creditors instead of having to bow and scrape to his patrons.'[27]

Svetlana Alpers proves convincingly that Rembrandt was out first and foremost to increase the market value of his art. At auctions he bought back many of his etchings at top prices. The most famous example of this is his etching *Christ Healing the Sick*, which he himself bought at an auction for 100 guilders and which to this very day is known as *The Hundred Guilder Print*. On this theme Alpers writes:

'thus it was ... Rembrandt who fostered the concept of art which has most influenced our culture - the concept of a commodity which is differentiated from other commodities in that it is not produced industrially, but in limited quantities, and creates its own market. In terms of its exceptional characteristics - the aura of individual authorship and resulting

Hendrickje at an Open Door, c. 1656. Canvas, 88.5 x 67 cm. Bredius 116
Berlin–Dahlem, Staatliche Museen, Gemäldegalerie

150

market value - that particular commodity "the work of art" is not too far removed from the more basic kinds found in an entrepreneurial venture (in the capitalist meaning of the word).'[28]

Rembrandt's policy of increasing the value of his works of art by reacquiring them at top prices cost him a fortune. This and the thoughtlessness with which he borrowed money are probably the reasons for his insolvency.

Even at the time of purchasing his house in 1639 Rembrandt was already in financial difficulties. The house in *Breestraat* which he was in the process of buying for Saskia and himself was to cost 13,000 guilders. Despite the huge sum of 40,700 guilders which Saskia had brought into the marriage, he was insolvent and could not afford the deposit of 1,200 guilders. It was then, after a long delay, that he finished his last two paintings for the stadtholder in The Hague, which brought in this very sum (cf. Chapter III, p. 73). On signing the sales contract for the house, he had promised to pay off the outstanding amount within the next five years, but in 1653 8,470.14 guilders still remained unpaid and the vendor's heir now planned to collect. On discovering this, Rembrandt borrowed a total of 9,180 guilders, which he promised to repay within a year, from several rich citizens of Amsterdam who were well disposed towards him. Even that was pie in the sky and the house was still not quite paid off; a residual debt of 1,000 guilders remained.

In 1655 he arranged through the orphans' court for his house to be made over to his son Titus in the hope that it would in this way escape the clutches of his creditors. This move proved pointless since as a result of Saskia's well-intentioned will Titus had no guardian other than Rembrandt. Had Saskia not made Rembrandt the sole guardian of their son then the orphans' court would have been forced after her death to compile an inventory of the items which made up Titus' rightful inheritance. Rembrandt would not have had access to this inheritance, but on the other hand his creditors would have had no claim upon it either. Now Rembrandt's creditors refused to leave the indebted painter alone and he knew of no other way out of the dispute than to ask the High Court in The Hague to grant him a so-called *cessio bonorum*, a sort of extension of credit. A *cessio bonorum* was granted to a citizen who found himself unable to pay his debts through no fault of his own. As grounds for the application Rembrandt stated that he had suffered losses on land and at sea. From this we can conclude that he was also involved as a sideline in transactions in the field of merchant shipping, which had suffered huge losses as a result of the naval war between England and the Netherlands between 1652 and 1654. Rembrandt's application for a *cessio bonorum*, which was granted, meant that as much of his property as was necessary to pay his creditors had to be auctioned, but on the other hand that he would not find himself in the debtors' prison. Should his property not raise the sum required, then creditors who had left empty-handed would not be able to take legal action against him again for a certain period. He would only have to meet the demands placed upon him after expiry of this period if he had capital of his own.

It was at this stage that the inventory which reveals exactly what Rembrandt owned was compiled. Apart from his own paintings, drawings and etchings, his collection included a fair number of pictures and graphic works by Dutch, Flemish, German and Italian masters, plaster casts of important sculptures, books, musical instruments, orientalia,

Hendrickje Bathing, 1655
Wood, 61.8 x 47 cm. Bredius 437
London, National Gallery

151

Titus, *c.* 1660
Canvas, 72 x 56 cm. Bredius 126
Paris, Musée du Louvre

weapons, armour, minerals, mouldings of flora and fauna, and also shells, stuffed animals and so on. The first auction took place in December 1657, but raised only 3,094 guilders. This sum bears no relation to the value of the collection and it appears that the buyers had agreed in advance to bid as little as possible. Next the house was compulsorily auctioned. It raised 2,000 guilders less than Rembrandt had originally bought it for. The final step was the auctioning of his collection of graphic art.

The total proceeds amounted to 15,000 guilders. This was not enough to satisfy Rembrandt's creditors and in addition Titus had lost his inheritance. Lawsuits filed by the various creditors followed. In 1665 the guardian who had in the meantime been appointed for Titus managed to obtain half the proceeds of the auction for his ward, which meant that one of the creditors had to repay the money which he had already received.

Following the move from *Breestraat* Hendrickje and Titus established

Hendrickje, 1660
Canvas, 78.4 x 68.9 cm
Bredius 118
New York, Metropolitan Museum
of Art, gift from Archer M.
Huntington in memory of Collis
Potter Huntington

an art dealership and formally took Rembrandt on as an employee. Everything which he produced belonged to them; the creditors had no rights to it. *De jure* Rembrandt worked for board and lodging and did not own a penny in his own right. *De facto* he was able to build up a new art collection, incur further debts, pawn paintings which were never finished and thus continue to owe his creditors the same large sums. Titus made efforts to obtain commissions, which Rembrandt then executed. As he had done during his time with Uylenburgh, he produced an extraordinary number of works. From this Svetlana Alpers concludes 'that Rembrandt found producing for the market for Uylenburgh and later for the family firm a welcome release from the pressures which dealing directly with patrons brought with it. In other words, he was at his most productive when he had nothing to do with them.'[29]

Rembrandt's financial conduct was interpreted in the main as incompetence in dealing properly with money. The question arises as to whether this interpretation is correct. The strategy which he employed enabled him to work with other people's money, buy himself a house without paying for it and use the money instead to build up an art collection and reacquire his own works in order to make them more valuable; for a long time this worked very well. Only after twenty years did the deliberate risk which he had taken result in his having to dispose of property which had never really belonged to him. He had seen through the principles of capitalism and acted accordingly. Having Hendrickje and

Floris Soop (1604-1657), 1654
Canvas, 140.3 x 114.9 cm
Bredius 275
New York, Metropolitan Museum,
Jules Bache Collection

Titus employ him in order that he might evade his creditors was just one example.

It is thus not appropriate to talk in terms of an impoverished artist who ten years before his death was alone, penniless and ill-used. Rembrandt always earned enough money to be able to lead a comfortable life. During the last decade of his life he created - relatively independently of patrons and the responsibilities of business, which were taken care of by Hendrickje and Titus - works which were to prove his most confident in terms of style and composition and which were totally independent of convention.

The later pictures

Rembrandt did not follow the stylistic changes which Dutch painting had undergone during the 1640s and he was now irrevocably an outsider. The final twenty years of his life were spent perfecting his own style and the compositional techniques which he had adopted over the years. Consequently, it is possible to see his later works as a continuation of his earlier career, even if insolvency and the consequent move to a modest house in a different neighbourhood had in the interim brought a change in his living conditions. This no longer affected his work. On the contrary, he was able to recapture the productivity of his best years. The themes remained the same. He continued to illustrate biblical histories and portraits. In a few cases the transition from one to the other was indistinct and researchers are unsure whether he painted a historical picture and made use of living models or whether he incorporated a family portrait into a historical scene, in other words painted a *portrait historiée*. The historical sources and the titles of the pictures do not offer any clues.

One example of a work which scarcely fits into either category is the

The Risen Christ Appearing to Mary Magdalene, 1651
Canvas, 65 x 79 cm. Bredius 583
Braunschweig, Herzog Anton–Ulrich–Museum

*Jacob Blessing
the Sons of Joseph*, 1656
Canvas, 175.5 x 210.5 cm
Bredius 525
Kassel, Staatliche
Kunstsammlungen

large painting *Jacob Blessing the Sons of Joseph* (ill. p. 156) from 1656. The story of Jacob comes from the Old Testament and tells how the aged Jacob travelled to Egypt with his eleven other sons to be reunited with his son Joseph, whom he had long believed to be dead. Jacob, who after his struggle with the angel was also known as Israel, and his sons remained in Egypt. In time their families grew larger until eventually they formed the twelve tribes which would subsequently go to make up the Israelite people. These tribes, which Moses later led from Egypt, bore the names of Jacob's twelve sons, who were designated the fathers of their tribes.

Rembrandt chose for his painting an event which took place during Jacob's lifetime. When Jacob realised that he was close to death Joseph brought his sons Manasseh and Ephraim to be blessed. The virtually blind old man laid his right hand on the younger Ephraim, for the purposes of which he had to cross his hands over, for Joseph had brought the children to him in such a way as to ensure that he would lay his right hand on Manasseh's head so that the first-born would receive the bless-

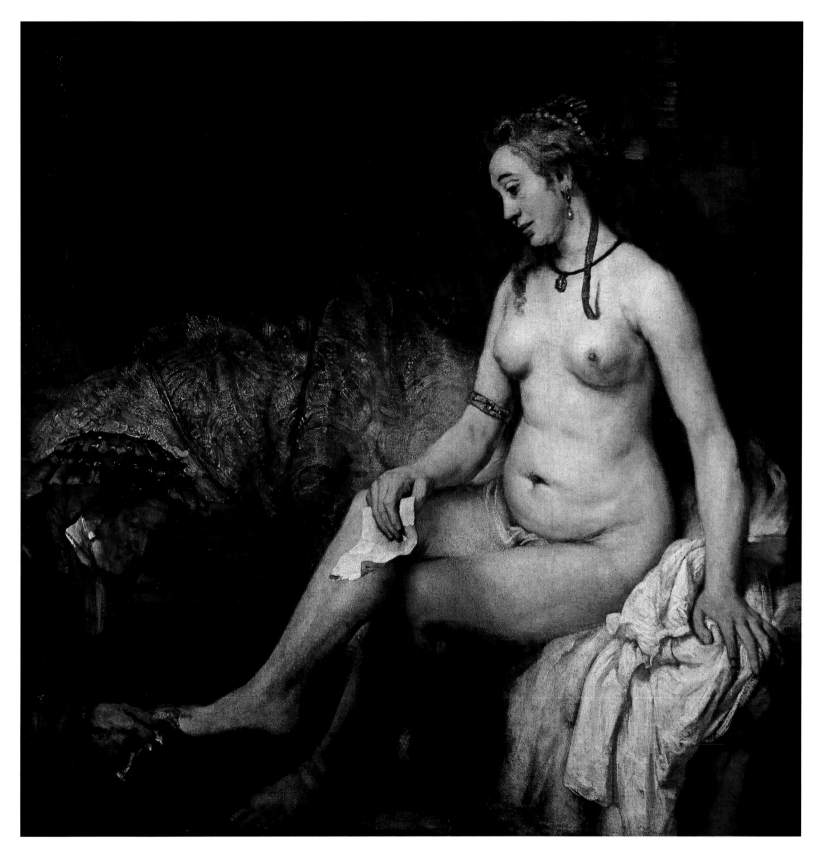

Bathsheba with King David's Letter, 1654
Canvas, 142 x 142 cm. Bredius 521
Paris, Musée du Louvre

ing which was his birthright. When Joseph pointed out his mistake Jacob explained that Ephraim would head a larger tribe than Manasseh. The Fathers of the Church interpreted this blessing as a prefiguration of Christianity. The actual blessing was granted to the newer Christian denomination and not to the Jews.

In his painting Rembrandt does not represent the theme in the traditional manner, that is with Jacob crossing over his hands. The blind old man has partially raised himself up and is leaning on his son's shoulder.

Moses with the Tablets of the Law, 1659
Canvas, 168.5 x 135.6 cm. Bredius 527
Berlin–Dahlem, Staatliche Museen, Gemäldegalerie

Joseph is supporting the hand with which his father is blessing Ephraim. With blond locks surrounded by an aura (halo), a golden yellow robe and his hands folded across his chest, Ephraim bears Christ's features. Manasseh is standing closer to his grandfather. His head just clears the coverlet and he appears smaller than his younger brother. Joseph is touching Manasseh's head with the hand which is supporting Jacob as if he wished to divert the blessing issuing from his father's right hand to himself. Of Jacob's other hand only three fingers are visible next to Manasseh's ear. This dark straight-haired boy is gazing with total impartiality at his brother and is completely unsuspecting.

Behind the two children stands Joseph's Egyptian wife Asenath, who is not mentioned at this point in the Bible. Both Joseph, who is bending down affectionately towards his father, and Asenath, who is gazing tenderly at her children, are clad in oriental robes. Nevertheless, the picture conveys not the pomp which was to be found in Rembrandt's paintings from the 1630s, but rather the intimacy of a family which has gathered around the dying father. On account of Asenath's presence in particular Gary Schwartz has claimed to see in the picture a family portrait and considers it possible to identify the family as that of Willem Schrijver.[30] Schrijver, the son of Petrus Scriverius, came from Leiden and became an alderman in 1656. In 1645 he had married Wendela de Graeff, who had two children from her first marriage. The son died at an early age; the daughter Alida survived her mother, who died in 1652, by four years. Willem Schrijver and Wendela de Graeff also had a son of their own. When Alida died in 1656 Willem Schrijver found himself in possession of a large fortune which he wanted to pass on to his son. There was a danger, however, that Wendela's first husband's family might also be able to enforce a claim on this inheritance. These fears of Willem's surfaced later and it is no longer possible to link them chronologically with Rembrandt's painting.

Schrijver had a 'large painting by Rembrandt hung over the fireplace', the title of which is not known.[31] Schwartz concludes from this and from Willem Schrijver's desire that his son, Wendela's second son, should have an inheritance - his title to which was not assured - that the picture is a family portrait legitimising these acquisitive interests. Schwartz thus identifies Jacob with Petrus Scriverius, who in 1656 was 80 years old, Joseph with Willem Schrijver, Asenath with the latter's deceased wife Wendela de Graeff, Manasseh with her likewise deceased son and Ephraim with Willem Schrijver's son. This identification cannot altogether be rejected out of hand, but the conclusion which Schwartz draws from his findings appears dubious: 'the implied interpretation of Rembrandt's great masterpiece brings it down to earth from the spiritual heights at which the subject is usually discussed ... [to] the earth on which Rembrandt's patrons were walking in 1656'.[32]

In contrast, Svetlana Alpers claims that Rembrandt obscured 'the distinction between those who paid to sit for their portraits and those models who were paid for it ... Although they paid Rembrandt for his services, he treated his customers not a jot or iota differently than his models, that is he did not regard them any differently than he regarded himself.'[33]

Irrespective of whether or not Gary Schwartz's interpretation is correct - something which, as Alpers' objection demonstrates, it is difficult to prove without precise details - we must not lose sight of the picture

Jacob Wrestling with the Angel, 1659
Canvas, 137 x 116 cm. Bredius 528
Berlin–Dahlem, Staatliche Museen, Gemäldegalerie

itself. Even if Schrijver did commission the picture on this theme from Rembrandt, it is clear from the way in which it is painted that the artist was actually concerned first and foremost with the interpretation of the biblical story and not the quarrels between Amsterdam citizens.

For other pictures the question of classification is more clear-cut. We know who Rembrandt's models were for paintings such as *Bathsheba with King David's Letter* of 1654 (ill. p. 157), but also know that Rembrandt was not concerned primarily to paint a portrait, but a historical picture. Rembrandt concentrated once again in these paintings on a particular moment in the plot and dispensed with details which seemed to him to spoil the picture's effect. One day, from the roof of his palace, King David sees a beautiful woman taking a bath. He enquires who she is and discovers that she is Bathsheba, the wife of the Hittite Uriah, who is away at war. David sends for her by letter and as a consequence she becomes pregnant, whereupon David attempts to induce Uriah to sleep with her in order to conceal his sin. When Uriah refuses to return to his wife because he does not want to forsake the other soldiers in the field, David has him moved to the front line, where he is killed.

Like that of Susannah, the story of Bathsheba was often used as a pretext for depicting a female nude. Bathsheba is generally pictured bathing and being watched by David. Rembrandt, however, decided upon a different scene. Bathsheba has already received David's letter and is being dressed ready to go to the palace. She is still naked. Her body is seen in bright light. A thin veil conceals only her most intimate parts. She is sitting on a bed, her head turned slightly to the side, and is looking down despondently at her maid, who is kneeling before her and beginning to dress her mistress. She too knows the content of the letter which Bathsheba holds in her hand. The bedroom setting hints at the consequences which Bathsheba's visit to David will have. Bathsheba realises that she cannot escape her destiny. Rembrandt knew how to show these feelings in her facial expression and it is contrasted with her naked body, which she is showing off and which has become her undoing.

Rembrandt's model for this painting was Hendrickje Stoffels, then his life companion. Just as Saskia and later Geertghe Dircx had sat for him, it was now Hendrickje who slipped into a variety of roles. However, her facial expression, pose and positioning in the picture, in short all that is required for an instinctive appreciation of a scene or person, were Rembrandt's own invention and had nothing to do with the person sitting for him. With this in mind, Svetlana Alpers' interpretation of the scene is dubious. She writes, 'Bathsheba's story was not dissimilar in certain respects to Hendrickje's own situation'.[34] She refers, of course, to the fact that Hendrickje had been branded a whore because of her relationship with Rembrandt and the child which she bore him in 1654 and was excluded from Holy Communion. But it is unlikely that this defamation prompted Rembrandt to draw parallels with the story of Bathsheba. Alpers has also put forward similar ideas about Saskia and her relationship with Rembrandt in connection with the painting *The Prodigal Son in a Bordello* (ill. p. 61). In doing so, however, she failed to consider Rembrandt's role as creator of the picture. He had often used his life companions as models for his paintings, but surely not with the intention of linking them with the figures depicted in those paintings. If nothing else, the fact that he painted them in a variety of totally different roles is proof of that. Besides, there are portraits enough of Hendrickje.

The Jewish Bride
(Isaac and Rebecca), c. 1662
Canvas, 121.5 x 166.5 cm
Bredius 416
Amsterdam, Rijksmuseum

Every attempt to explain Rembrandt the man and his relationships with women in particular through his pictures has so far failed.

Equally dubious is the theory that it was the commissions for the decoration of the City Hall - which had been awarded shortly before and one of whose themes was the story of Moses - which inspired him to paint the picture *Moses with the Tablets of the Law* (ill. p. 158) in 1659. Chapter 32 of the Book of Exodus tells how Moses leaves the Israelites alone in the wilderness and holds a dialogue with God on Mount Sinai. When he is away too long the people are stricken with doubts and demand an image which they can worship. Aaron, the high priest and brother of Moses, has a golden calf cast out of the women's jewellery for

them to venerate. In the midst of the ceremony, the dance and the veneration of the Golden Calf, Moses returns from Mount Sinai with the tablets into which God has cut the Ten Commandments which the tribe is to follow. When Moses sees that the Israelites have deviated from the true faith and are worshipping an image he smashes the tablets in rage. He subsequently returns to Mount Sinai for forty days and forty nights and is given the Commandments a second time; they have since formed the major foundation of Jewish and Christian concepts of morality.

Rembrandt did not depict the dance around the Golden Calf, a theme which artists keenly depicted time and time again well into the classical modern age. By singling out a salient moment and the internal tension which determines it as such, he concentrates totally on the figure of Moses. The leader of the Israelites stands in front of a couple of rocks representing the descent from Sinai. Because he is rendered only in half-length the picture is dominated by his arms, with which he holds the heavy decalogue above his head in order to hurl it to the ground the next moment. His actions contrast with his facial expression, which reflects not anger but sadness and resignation. As in the painting of Bathsheba, his pose and facial expression do not tally and thus demonstrate the conflict of human emotions. In this relatively lightly coloured picture with its yellowish, greenish and brownish tones the black tablets stand out in stark contrast. The last five Commandments are cut into the tablet at the front in Hebrew script. Moses' face and arms are bathed in a bright light. Two curls on his forehead resemble horns. In this respect Rembrandt's depiction was in keeping with the iconographic tradition for the depiction of Moses. Whilst translating the Bible into Latin, one of the Fathers of the Church, St Jerome (c. 347-420) made the mistake of translating the Hebrew word for 'to shine' with the word 'horned'. Since then Moses has been represented with two horns growing out of his forehead. Even before Rembrandt, these horns had been toned down through their replacement by two horn-like locks of hair. Rembrandt adopted this modification.

Similar in construction to the Moses painting is the painting *Jacob Wrestling with the Angel* (ill. p. 160), also dated 1659. It recounts the story of Jacob, who is forced to flee after paying his twin brother Esau a mess of potage for the blessing which is Esau's birthright and only returns with his wife Rachel, twelve children and a relatively large fortune after thirteen years. Once he has calmed his brother's fury with generous gifts and is able to cross the ford, the angel of the Lord appears to Jacob at night in the form of an unknown man and wrestles with him until he dislocates Jacob's thigh. When morning breaks and the angel wishes to free himself from the clasp Jacob says, 'I will not let thee go, except thou bless me',[35] whereupon the angel blesses him and gives him the name Israel, meaning 'God's fighter'. The canvas of Rembrandt's painting has been cut down slightly, but it is safe to assume that the painting contained nothing extra. Once again nothing other than the landscape is sketched in the background. Jacob is depicted in half-length and has turned his back to the beholder. The angel is depicted face-on. He is clasping one of Jacob's thighs between his legs and with his left hand he has clasped Jacob around the waist. Accordingly, the struggle appears to be over and the angel seems already to have dislocated Jacob's thigh, hence perhaps Jacob's slightly distorted pose. Tümpel may well be correct when he claims that Rembrandt's painting does not depict the

*Ahasuerus and Haman
at Esther's Feast*, 1660
Canvas, 73 x 94 cm. Bredius 530
Moscow, Pushkin Museum

actual struggle, but the moment of the blessing. Once again Rembrandt has selected as his subject a somewhat different point in the story than that generally depicted. Although he returned time and time again to traditional, well-known themes, his work was nevertheless innovative to the extent that he selected different moments from the plot, which although linked to the more frequently depicted scenes nevertheless required new designs.

In the 1950s it was correctly pointed out that the painting had a perplexing component. The perplexity is caused by the painting's tendency to eroticism. Rembrandt painted the angel with the features of a very pretty young man and emphasised his sensuous mouth. In his right arm he holds Jacob's head, with his hand he clasps Jacob tenderly around the neck. He is gazing affectionately at Jacob, whose eyes are half-closed. The upper part of Jacob's body is resting on the angel's thigh; Jacob's clasp could also be interpreted as an embrace. God's blessing and thus God's love as represented by the angel have been brought down to a human level. Love is linked with eroticism. Eroticism is thus not limited to the relationship between man and woman. With this picture Rembrandt proved his ability to represent the ambivalence of human emotions in a way not previously seen.

Haman Recognises his Fate, c. 1660
Canvas, 127 x 117 cm. Bredius 531
Leningrad, Hermitage

The Apostle Peter
Denying Christ, 1660
Canvas, 154 x 169 cm. Bredius 594
Amsterdam, Rijksmuseum

Some years later he returned to the theme of eroticism. In a famous half-length from his later period, the so-called *Jewish Bride* (ill. p. 162) from 1666, Rembrandt depicted the relationship between man and wife. Just recently another argument has arisen about the designation of the picture. Since the nineteenth century the figures in the picture have been identified as a Jewish father releasing his daughter from the parental home into marriage. Tümpel has been able to show convincingly that the couple are Isaac and Rebecca, who passed themselves off to the Philistines as brother and sister, but were observed in romantic embrace by King Abimelech, who then called Isaac to account. As the model for the picture Tümpel gives a reproduction engraving after a fresco by Raphael in which two figures appear in similar pose. Rembrandt, however, did not incorporate the figure of Abimelech into the composition, but depicted only the lovers.

Schwartz has another interpretation. He links the painting with a stage play performed frequently in Amsterdam during the 1660s and sees in the lovers the play's chief protagonists, Cyrus and Aspasia. He substantiates his claim that the two figures could not be Jews, saying, 'when I visited the Rijksmuseum several years ago with the old Jewish mother of a friend, who also knew what she was talking about, she commented, after scrutinising the couple's behaviour, "They're not Jewish".'[36] Like Alpers' interpretation of the Bathsheba painting, this interpretation once again neglects the painter. Rembrandt was neither a behavioural scientist nor an ethnologist. When he selected a theme from the Old Testament he was hardly likely to study the rules of conduct which applied to seventeenth-century Jews; instead he almost certainly intended to use the theme to point out universal forms of human behaviour. Like Tümpel, however, Schwartz ascertains that the couple could not be father and daughter, but must represent lovers.

Attempts to see the picture as an official double portrait (the couple have been linked, for instance, with Titus and his wife Magdalena van Loo) have not as yet proved convincing. As with the painting *Jacob Blessing the Sons of Joseph* (cf. p. 156), Alpers has been able to make out a case for her claim that Rembrandt often made no distinction between the portraits which he painted of his contemporaries and the depiction of historical figures and that it is therefore scarcely possible to identify pictures as portraits unless they are proven to be such by the historical sources.

The way in which the two figures in the painting are made to relate to

Jacob Trip (1575–1661), c. 1661
Canvas, 130.5 x 97 cm. Bredius 314
London, National Gallery

Marguerite de Geer (1583–1672), 1661
Canvas, 130.5 x 97.5 cm
Bredius 394
London, National Gallery

The Evangelist Matthew, 1661
Canvas, 96 x 81 cm. Bredius 614
Paris, Musée du Louvre

The Apostle Simon, 1661
Canvas, 98.3 x 79 cm
Bredius–Gerson 616A
Zurich, Kunsthaus, Ruzicka
Foundation

each other has led researchers to revise the old title *The Jewish Bride*.

Characteristically for his later works, Rembrandt has chosen here to use half-lengths which take up the whole height of the picture. The woman is sitting on the man's lap. He has turned to her and laid one arm around her shoulder, his right hand rests on her left breast. She is touching his hand tenderly with her fingertips; her other hand rests in her lap and thus points to her more intimate parts. The hands, which often play an important part in Rembrandt's work, express all. Because of the unambiguity with which the man and woman express their desires here, the erotic component is not as subtle as in the painting *Jacob Wrestling with the Angel* (ill. p. 160). The two pictures share a tranquillity which is inconsistent with their content. In one case this tranquillity emphasises the moment after the struggle; in the other it serves to check the figures' desire. Had Rembrandt made *The Jewish Bride* more erotic then he would certainly have come into conflict with his patrons. The theme of *Jacob Wrestling with the Angel*, on the other hand, was ostensibly quite different, although the picture was always open to reinterpretation, with the result that in that picture Rembrandt was able to be more daring.

Rembrandt frequently interpreted figures from the Bible in a new way. Moses, for instance, was depicted not in a fury but sorrowful and resigned. In the painting *Haman Recognises his Fate* (ill. p. 165) from

169

The Circumcision of Christ, 1661
Canvas, 56.5 x 75 cm. Bredius 596
Washington, National Gallery of
Art, Widener Collection

*The Return of the
Prodigal Son*, c. 1668–1669
Canvas, 262 x 206 cm. Bredius 598
Leningrad, Hermitage

around 1660 Rembrandt altered the figure of Haman more radically still. Haman was adviser to the Persian king Ahasuerus and wanted to have all the Jews still in Babylon, which had fallen to Persia, killed. For his adversary Mordecai, who had prevented an assassination attempt on Ahasuerus and refused to kneel before Haman, Haman had a high gallows built. His plan was thwarted by Esther, the king's wife, herself a Jewess. She invited Ahasuerus and Haman to dine with her (ill. p. 164) and during the course of the conversation posed such clever questions that Haman betrayed himself and suffered the death which he had planned for Mordecai, who was also Esther's foster father and adviser. In his painting Rembrandt does not depict Haman as a vain courtier - as was usual - but as a humbled, pitiable man. Still clad in the splendid robes which he will soon have to hand over to Mordecai, he stands with his eyes closed. His right hand rests on his breast as if he were repenting of his sins. The king and Mordecai, whose heads in the background frame the figure of Haman, do not look triumphant, but rather pensive, sympathetic and sorrowful. One cannot avoid comparison with the repentant Judas whom Rembrandt had painted in 1629 (ill. p. 38). In both pictures the painter's objective was to represent the feeling of remorse.

However, the pictures also demonstrate the extent to which Rembrandt had moved on from his beginnings and how much more powerfully his later pictures appeal to the emotions of the beholder through their concentration on the essential features. Nor did Rembrandt

171

only tackle stories from the Old Testament in this later phase. Events from the New Testament also continued to play an important part in his paintings. With the help of his pupils, for instance, he painted a series of pictures depicting the apostles and evangelists. Since he involved his studio in the execution of this project, the three evangelists and nine apostles which we know today have several different qualities about them. One of the most beautiful of these pictures is the painting of the evangelist Matthew (ill. p. 168) from 1661. Matthew is sitting at a desk. In one hand he holds the quill which he is using to write down the gospel in the large volume which lies opened before him. He is depicted as an old man with a full beard. His wrinkled face matches his hands, whose veins stand out boldly. Behind him we see the head of an angel, the symbol of Matthew since time out of mind. Here the angel has been incorporated into the action and is thus not recognisable at first glance as a symbol. The angel has laid one hand on the evangelist's shoulder and appears to be dictating the text to him. His half-opened mouth is close to Matthew's ear and Matthew has turned his head, almost imperceptibly, towards the angel and is listening attentively. For the moment he is still listening, but directly he will start to write again and commit the divine message to paper.

Rembrandt clearly used the same model for the figure of the angel in this picture as he had used for the angel in *Jacob Wrestling with the Angel* (cf. p. 160). The suggestion that in both cases the model was his son Titus (ill. p. 152) cannot be rejected out of hand, but Rembrandt has changed his son's features somewhat, especially around the mouth.

In one of his last pictures we can once again see clearly how much importance Rembrandt placed upon the expression of emotion. In the painting *The Return of the Prodigal Son* (ill. p. 170) from 1668/69 Rembrandt depicts the moment at which the now guilt-ridden son, having squandered his inheritance, is taken into his father's arms in a gesture of forgiveness. The father's strength vests totally in his hands, which he has rested on the shoulders of his son - who is kneeling before him - in what is to all intents and purposes a blessing.

In his later pictures Rembrandt abandoned the precise painting techniques which had been characteristic of his work during the 1630s in favour of very much more hazy, often expressive brush strokes. He now made use in his historical pictures of the stylistic devices which he had developed in his landscape paintings, albeit not quite so consistently. In his choice of theme he continued to look to his old teacher Pieter Lastman, although this has only recently been recognised as a consequence of his tendency to disengage individual figures or groups of people from the greater composition, and as a result some of the pictures have acquired new titles, mainly with the help of Tümpel. Working in this way required Rembrandt to know in detail all the artistic sources available and traditional ways of illustrating a subject as well as to study the appropriate texts. In some of his final commissions his learnedness, which has repeatedly been called into question, is once again clearly in evidence.

The final commissions

Simeon's Song of Praise, c. 1661
Canvas, 98 x 79 cm. Bredius 600
Stockholm, Nationalmuseum

Rembrandt accepted commissions for portraits right up until his death - in all probability this was one of his most secure sources of income.

Aristotle with a
Bust of Homer, 1653
Canvas, 143.5 x 136.5 cm
Bredius 478
New York, Metropolitan Museum of Art

Homer, 1663
Canvas, 108 x 82.4 cm. Bredius 483
The Hague, Mauritshuis

Though he was known for his long sittings and unreliability in meeting deadlines, his portraits were still highly thought of during the 1650s and 1660s. He generally found it most difficult to meet deadlines when working on larger commissions, especially those for historical pictures. Nor did his behaviour change later. If a patron criticised, or even wished to make changes, the painter would become highly irritated. He did not comply with the conditions which his customers imposed on him, but instead offended them. He never negotiated when it came to fees. If a patron was not willing to pay the sum requested then he would rather do without than yield. It was he and not the buyers who determined his market value. Rembrandt's behaviour is best illustrated by the story of a commission which he began in 1653 but did not complete until the 1660s. His customer was a Sicilian.

During the 1650s Rembrandt had made a name for himself far beyond the borders of the Netherlands. This is confirmed in an expression of gratitude addressed to the painter and written in the 1650s by the poet Jeremias de Decker (1609-1666), whom Rembrandt was painting shortly before his death (ill. p. 177):

'And to secure your famous name with rhyme, is to carry water to the sea or wood to the forest ... This noble brush ... is famous by its own

Alexander the Great, 1655
Canvas, 137.5 x 104.4 cm
Bredius 480
Glasgow, Art Gallery and
Museum

devices and may have borne the name of its master as far as Dutch ships sail. His fame as an artist, which has crossed the peaks of the Alps and pushed as far as glorious Rome, makes even Italy look up inspired from the banks of the Tiber. For it moves thousands there to strike the flag before him. There one can of course compare his brushstrokes to those of Raphael and Michelangelo, indeed, he outstrips them.'[37]

Though this may have been a case of a friend exaggerating the painter's fame, that friend was nevertheless correct in suggesting that Rembrandt was not only well known in Italy but also highly thought of there. In 1653 the Sicilian aristocrat Don Antonio Ruffo, who owned a large art collection containing paintings by renowned European artists such as Dürer, Titian, Jordaens, Anthony van Dyck, Lucas van Leyden, Nicolas Poussin and Jusepe de Ribera, ordered a painting from Rembrandt which was to depict a historical figure at half-length. The theme of the commission was not specified more precisely; the painter was to have a free hand. Rembrandt decided on a depiction of the Greek philosopher Aristotle (ill. p. 174), and this he delivered in 1654. Ruffo was enthusiastic and ordered two further, complementary pictures from Rembrandt. By 1660, however, he had still not heard a word from Amsterdam and turned with his request for a counterpart to the *Aristotle* to the Italian painter

Jeremias de Decker
(1609–1666), 1666
Wood, 71 x 56 cm. Bredius 320
Leningrad, Hermitage

Guercino (1591-1666). Guercino declared his willingness and also referred in the written response which contained his acceptance to Ruffo's utterances on the subject of the *Aristotle*, saying:

'As for the half-figure of Rembrandt which has come into your hands, it cannot be other than complete perfection, because I have seen various works of his in prints which have come to our region. They are very beautiful in execution ... and done in a fine manner, so that one can assume that his work in colour is likewise of complete exquisiteness and perfection. I sincerely esteem him as a great artist.'[38] This assessment from an Italian fellow-painter shows just how well known Rembrandt was in Italy by then.

In the meantime Rembrandt too had begun work on Ruffo's commission. In 1661 he completed the painting *Alexander the Great* and in 1662 he delivered his picture of the Greek poet, *Homer* (ill. p. 175). Ruffo did not approve of either. He criticised the fact that parts of the *Alexander* canvas were added on and claimed that the *Homer* was only half-finished. In addition, Rembrandt was demanding a completely exorbitant fee, which he was not prepared to pay. Rembrandt responded confidently to the criticism of the *Alexander*, saying 'I am wholly amazed at the way in which you have written about the *Alexander*, which is painted so extraordinarily well. I cannot believe that there are many art-lovers in

The Conspiracy of
Claudius Civilis, 1661–1662
Canvas, 196 x 309 cm. Bredius 482
Stockholm, Nationalmuseum

Messina.[39] He explained to Ruffo that it was not until he had already begun the painting that he realised that he had selected too small a canvas. If, he said, Ruffo were to hang the picture in the right light then the seams, which had been painted over very well, would not be visible. He was not prepared to discuss the fee of 500 guilders per picture, despite the fact that in Amsterdam too he would have got only a fraction of the sum which he was asking of Ruffo for paintings of this kind. Ruffo declared

The Conspiracy of Claudius Civilis,
End of 1661
Drawing, 19.6 x 18 cm
Benesch 1061
Munich, Graphische Sammlung

himself satisfied with the *Alexander*, but sent the *Homer* back.
Rembrandt painted in another two scribes, who were recording the
words of the blind poet, and in 1663 returned the painting once more to
Ruffo. These minor characters were later obliterated by a fire in which
the picture was damaged.

Rembrandt's behaviour indicates a self-assured artist who recognised
how well he was known and exploited this unashamedly. His insolvency

*The Syndics of the Drapers' Guild
(De Staalmeester)*, 1661
Canvas, 191.5 x 279 cm
Bredius 415
Amsterdam, Rijksmuseum

had brought no radical change in his self-appreciation. The commission from Ruffo was, however, not merely important for the documentary evidence which it provided. The pictures show just how flexible Rembrandt could be in his choice of theme: at the time that he was concentrating on stories from the Bible he also turned to figures from classical history and developed a new programme.

In the first of the pictures which Rembrandt painted for Ruffo (ill. p. 174), Aristotle stands against a dark background. He is dressed in black; only his illuminated face, yellow coat and chain of honour stand out clearly. He has laid one hand on a bust of Homer, which stands next to him, and with the other he is touching the chain of honour. On this chain hangs a medallion containing a portrait of Alexander the Great,

which is to be found between Homer's head and that of Aristotle. Rembrandt's bust of Homer was modelled on a Hellenistic sculpture which had become well known from casts. He later painted Homer and Alexander the Great - who in the picture are united through the treatment - individually again (ill. p. 176). Ruffo's picture of Alexander the Great has not survived, but was probably not dissimilar to the *Alexander* shown here.

The message contained in the three paintings suggests that Rembrandt studied in detail historical references to the three figures and their significance to Calvinism. Aristotle was regarded as an authority on and interpreter of Homer's writings and acquainted his pupil Alexander with these. It is said that Alexander always carried the books of the old poet with him during his campaigns. Moreover, to the Calvinists these three figures from ancient Greece were symbolic. Aristotle represented scholarliness (philosophy), Homer genius (the art of poetry) and Alexander the effective action of a ruler. Hence in this one picture, the *Aristotle*, which was planned as a depiction of a historical figure, Rembrandt combined classical scholarliness with contemporary theological references. He then expanded this idea by painting two further pictures, the content of which referred back to the first. The commission allowed him so much latitude that he was able to put his own ideas into effect. It is noteworthy that although he had hardly ever before tackled classical themes (and was to abandon them totally in his later years), when he received this commission from a Sicilian he took up classical ideas, which were much more widespread in Italy, but invested them with Calvinist substance.

Rembrandt's self-confidence sprang from an awareness of his talents, which were not merely compositional and stylistic, but also based on an appreciation of historical interconnections and their significance for his own age.

Rembrandt's success both in persuading his Sicilian patron to accept his ideas and in demanding a disproportionately large sum of money of him was not echoed in his native land. Let us look, for example, at the commission which he received for the City Hall in Amsterdam. In 1648, the year in which the Netherlands at last officially became an independent republic, building began on the new City Hall. The building was to symbolise the republican form of government and thus also to be a monument to liberty. It was to follow in the tradition of the city halls built in the free cities of Italy during the fourteenth century and, as was the case in Italy, the sumptuous decorations were to attract attention to the fine government, which guaranteed the people affluence, peace and liberty. The burgomasters of the city awarded commissions for the decoration of the City Hall to various Amsterdam artists, mostly pupils of Rembrandt; at first, however, their teacher was not considered.

The most important part of this public programme was the civic hall. Twelve monumental paintings were planned for this room, the theme of which was to be the Batavian uprising. The Batavian tribe, which had lived on Dutch territory under Roman rule and which in AD 69-70 attempted to rise up and regain its liberty, was the tribe on which the free republic liked to model itself. As far back as the beginning of the seventeenth century the Batavians were regarded as the forefathers of the Dutch, one result of which, for example, was that the Dutch named their trade centre in Java (today Djakarta) Batavia.

A Family Likeness, c. 1663–1668
Canvas, 126 x 167 cm. Bredius 417
Braunschweig, Herzog Anton–
Ulrich–Museum

In 1659 Govert Flinck was awarded the commission for these twelve paintings, but when he died in 1660 he had made few drafts and the city fathers had to find new painters to complete the job. They decided upon Jan Lievens, who was by then also resident in Amsterdam, Jacob Jordaens from Antwerp and Rembrandt. Rembrandt was to paint the first picture, *The Conspiracy of Claudius Civilis* (ill. p. 178). For this he must have read Tacitus, for he kept relatively closely to this source. He painted Claudius Civilis just as the Roman historian had described him - blind in one eye - and set the scene around midnight. The oath is sealed not with a handshake but with the crossing of swords and is thus a Batavian oath.

Only a fragment of this monumental painting, which was once square and almost six metres in length, has survived. The only clue we have as to its size and composition is a small sketch which Rembrandt did on the reverse of a letter announcing someone's death (ill. p. 179):

'Only with the help of our imaginations can we visualise how this harshly lit, barbaric conspiratorial group must have appeared out of the dark, secret surroundings like a scene illuminated by spotlights on a stage - a stage high up under an arch in the gallery of the City Hall. One can only describe Rembrandt's composition as fascinatingly dramatic.'[40]

In 1661 Rembrandt delivered the huge painting, and in 1662, according to a description of Amsterdam by Melchior Fokkens, it was hanging in place. But before August 1662 the painting was returned to Rembrandt for retouching. Since he did not complete the picture in time for the next state visit, Govert Flinck's sketch was transformed into an oil painting within four days. Rembrandt had asked for an increased fee for retouching the painting. He did not, however, receive it. From his stubborn behaviour towards Ruffo when the latter attempted to force down the fee we may conclude that he refused to return the painting unless the sum requested was paid. Now he received no money at all for it and also had a bulky picture taking up valuable space in his studio. He reduced the canvas to its present size, 196 x 309 cm, and altered the picture. Had Rembrandt retouched and returned the painting within a reasonable length of time and without demanding further money, it would probably still be hanging in the place for which it was intended. His pride and his image of himself did not permit that. He preferred to do without a fee completely rather than to allow himself to be forced into doing work for which he would not be paid.

Whilst still working on the commission for the City Hall, or shortly after its delivery, Rembrandt was commissioned by the drapers to paint a group portrait. Every year on Good Friday the drapers' guild selected five sampling officials to assess the quality of the textiles which were produced in Amsterdam. They met several times a week in the guildhall to do their job.

In 1763 six group portraits hung in the room in which these sampling officials met; the oldest was from 1559 and all were painted to the same pattern. Around this time the Amsterdam historian Jan Wagenaar described the paintings, saying, 'In each of these paintings are portrayed five wardens seated and the *Staalhof* steward, standing'.[41] Rembrandt also followed this tradition (ill. p. 180), although probably only with reluctance. An X-ray of the painting shows that he first painted the syndic at the front standing. In all probability this led to protests from the other four, and Rembrandt subsequently painted him in a half-standing, half-sitting pose which with good will can be interpreted as meaning that he is in the process of sitting down. Earlier researchers suggested something to the effect that the *Staalmeesters* are in discussion with an undepicted public. Recently it has been suggested that the book lying before them on the table contains the patterns of the materials which they are responsible for sampling. Even allowing for this, Rembrandt followed tradition more in this painting than ever before. Only through the poses, facial expressions and gestures of the five syndics and the *Staalhof* steward, who is visible in the background without a hat, does the picture acquire a liveliness which the other group portraits lack.

The final years

In 1663, only a few years after Rembrandt had sold his house in *Breestraat* and become an employee in the art dealership owned by Hendrickje and Titus, his life companion died (their daughter Cornelia was then 9 years old). Titus continued to manage his father's business affairs and in 1665 he was finally paid the inheritance to which he was entitled from the insolvent's estate, albeit 13,000 guilders less than he should have received. In the same year he came of age. Saskia's relatives,

Self–portrait, 1657
Canvas, 53.5 x 44 cm. Bredius 48
Edinburgh, National Gallery of
Scotland (on loan from the Duke
of Sutherland)

the Uylenburghs, continued to remind Rembrandt that he owed them money and it is therefore entirely possible that his father's influence had something to do with Titus' marriage in February 1668 to Magdalena van Loo, who was related to them. In this way Saskia's fortune, which Titus had inherited, found its way back into the family. Rembrandt was finally left in peace by his creditors.

In September 1668 Titus died. Magdalena was expecting a child. When her daughter Titia was born in March 1669 Rembrandt was appointed as her godfather. Six months later Titia lost her mother. Rembrandt himself died on 4 October 1669 and was buried four days later. The Guild of St Luke buried with him a commemoration medal. The furnishings and fittings listed in the inventory of his household compiled by a notary the day after his death were nothing like as valuable as those from *Breestraat*. Over the last ten years Rembrandt had lived more modestly. Nevertheless, three rooms had been reserved for the art collection which he had rebuilt. This contained paintings, drawings, curiosities and antiques. The notion of an artist so poor that he broke open his 15-year-old daughter's piggy-bank in order that he could buy something to eat must be condemned to the realm of legend. Rembrandt certainly did not die in poverty.

Nor indeed was he ever forgotten or unappreciated during his lifetime.

Self–portrait, 1658
Canvas, 133.7 x 103.8 cm
Bredius 50
New York, The Frick Collection

The laughing painter

Rembrandt's late self-portraits show, with unsparing candour, the decline of a person in old age. At the same time they also reflect the unbroken self-confidence of this artist. If we compare the portraits from 1657 and 1658, we see that in the later picture the face has become older and more puffy. Though Rembrandt was just 52 years old when it was painted, it is the face of an old man. Yet despite his age he has not abandoned his majestic pose. Sumptuously dressed, he depicts himself more or less in

Self–portrait as
the Apostle Paul, 1661
Canvas, 91 x 77 cm. Bredius 59
Amsterdam, Rijksmuseum

the role of a ruler. He is not seated but throned and looking straight ahead and out of the picture. One hand rests on the arm of the chair, in the other he holds a stick which could perhaps also be interpreted as a ruler's insignia.

In 1661 Rembrandt painted himself in the role of the apostle Paul (ill. p. 186). The picture is linked to his series of apostles and evangelists. As in the earlier portraits, he has set himself at a diagonal in the picture and is turning his head in such a way that he looks straight ahead at the beholder. In his hands he is holding a book containing Hebrew script, which has been interpreted as the Old Testament. Protruding from his coat is the pommel of a sword, the symbol of the apostle, and he has wrapped a turban around his head from beneath which his curls grow. His gaze as he looks out of the picture is questioning, with raised eyebrows and knitted forehead. There is nothing apostolic or indeed lordly about this face; it is the face of a man of experience who is sceptical about the future.

In one of his last self-portraits (ill. p. 189) Rembrandt again depicted himself as a painter. He is standing before an easel, on which he has painted a serious, almost gloomy-looking man. The easel has been cut out almost completely; we see only the nose, mouth and eyes of the painted likeness. Rembrandt, however, is not looking at his work but gazing out of the picture and laughing. This laugh has prompted many different interpretations. Whilst Gary Schwartz has adopted Albert Blankert's theory that the painting depicts Rembrandt in the role of the Greek painter Zeuxis, who is laughing himself to death as he paints a curious-looking old woman,[42] Tümpel puts forward the theory that the artist is depicted in the role of the Greek philosopher Democritus. The picture on the easel would then be of Heraclitus. Democritus and Heraclitus were regarded as opposites, the laughing philosopher and the grim, sobbing philosopher, and the couple were depicted frequently in the baroque period. Both pondered the transience of the world, one calmly and cheerfully, the other bitterly and sobbing. There are arguments in support of both interpretations, but they also have their weaknesses. The fact that Rembrandt portrayed himself here as a painter would appear to favour the Zeuxis theory. On the other hand, Zeuxis did not paint a gloomy-looking man, but a curious old woman. Then again, the fact that Rembrandt's painting does not depict him as a philosopher counts against the Democritus theory. The decisive factor is the manner in which Rembrandt is laughing in the self-portrait. It is not the kind of laugh which might lead to death. Rembrandt is not depicted 'caught in the jaws of death',[43] but as an old painter making fun of the person opposite, the beholder. He is adopting for himself - the laughing painter - the *Weltanschauung* of Democritus, whose cheerful, imperturbable outlook clearly left its mark on his teachings on the nature of things.[44] What we see here, then, is an old man depicting himself as an ugly greybeard; he has achieved a great deal during his lifetime but although he has long passed the height of his fame he does not doubt his own ability. The thickly applied paint leaves the face looking more wrinkled, more emaciated than it was in reality (ill. p. 188). The facial expression and the bushy, raised eyebrows add a sinister touch to the face.

Back in 1629 Rembrandt had depicted himself as a young man (ill. p. 8). His gaze at that time was questioning and searching. His life still lay before him and so too did his hopes of success. Once this success had

Self–portrait, 1669
Canvas, 86 x 70.5 cm. Bredius 55
London, National Gallery

been achieved, at the height of his fame in 1640, he depicted himself in aristocratic pose (ill. p. 106): a handsome, sumptuously dressed man with regular features and a steady gaze. A little less than thirty years after this the painter is still capable of depicting himself representatively; he remains confident of his position as an artist but now the wisdom of old age has also given him the ability to laugh at both himself and the world.

24 Hamann 1905 (³1920, p. 12ff.)

25 Schwartz 1985, p. 283

26 Alpers 1989, p. 206

27 ibid., p. 207

28 ibid., p. 244

29 ibid., p. 201

30 Schwartz 1985, p. 269ff.

31 ibid., p. 269

32 ibid., p. 271

33 Alpers 1989, p. 195f.

34 ibid., p. 185

35 Genesis (first book of Moses), Chapter 32, Verse 26

36 Schwartz 1985, p. 328

37 Cit. in Tümpel 1986, p. 361

38 ibid. (also in Rosenberg 1980, p. 281)

39 ibid., p. 363

40 Haak 1984, p. 363

41 Cit. in Schwartz 1985, p. 336

42 Schwartz 1985, p. 354ff.

43 ibid., p. 354

44 cf. also Tümpel 1986, p. 368

Self–portrait as Democritus, c. 1669
Canvas, 82.5 x 65 cm. Bredius 61
Cologne, Wallraf–Richartz–Museum

Chapter VI

Research and the problem of attribution

At the end of the nineteenth century a Swiss family offered for sale a picture held to be a genuine Rembrandt. The painting, which was in need of restoration, showed the head of a man wearing a golden helmet. Quite by chance the painting was acquired in 1897 by the erstwhile director of the Berlin picture gallery. After its restoration it came to be regarded as a portrait of Rembrandt's brother Adriaen. Soon it was one of the most famous pictures in Berlin, was reproduced in large numbers as a postcard and was an established part of a general education, even to the point of its being used in reading books in schools. When art historians dated the painting to the mid-1650s (the picture is neither signed nor dated) the notion that it might be a portrait of Rembrandt's brother was given up and it acquired the title *The Man with the Golden Helmet* (ill. p. 190). Not until the beginning of the 1970s did researchers identify it as *Mars after the Falling Silent of the Weapons*.

In 1985 this famous picture, which year after year had captivated large numbers of visitors to Berlin's museums, hit the headlines. Careful scientific studies had allegedly proved that the picture had not been painted by Rembrandt himself. In art history circles speculation had been rife since 1969 that this famous painting was not from the hand of the great Dutch master, but by a pupil. X-rays and examinations using infra-red light gave no clear indications. Next the Berlin scientists turned to their colleagues in the field of physics to produce an autoradiograph of the picture with the help of an atomic reactor so that the several layers of paint could be studied in detail. It took physicists three years to prepare their atomic reactor for this purpose in collaboration with restorers and art historians. The results are now known. *The Man with the Golden Helmet* is not a Rembrandt, but by one of his pupils. Which of the numerous assistants from Rembrandt's studio was responsible is not known.

The evidence led to a reassessment of the picture. At the end of the last century the painting was highly praised for the first time when art historian Ferdinand Laban spoke of the 'stupendous bravura of the artistic structure', of 'boldness and subtlety of effect' and of 'artistic precision'. In 1948, in his great monograph on Rembrandt, Jacob Rosenberg assessed the picture as follows:

'A few words cannot do justice to this masterpiece, which modern critics have especially praised for the boldness of Rembrandt's technique in the powerful impasto of the helmet. ... The contrast between the splendour of the helmet and the subdued tonality of the face makes one deeply conscious of both the tangible and the intangible forces in Rembrandt's world, and of their inseparable inner relationship. As in all his greatest works, one feels here a fusion of the real with the visionary, and this

'Rembrandt'
*The Man with
the Golden Helmet*, *c.* 1650
Canvas, 67 x 50 cm. Bredius 128
Berlin–Dahlem, Staatliche Museen,
Gemäldegalerie

'Rembrandt'
David Playing the
Harp before Saul, 1655
Canvas, 130 x 164.3 cm
Bredius 526
The Hague, Mauritshuis

painting, through its inner glow and its deep harmonies, comes closer to the effect of music than to that of the plastic arts.'[45]

Today voices are being raised in disagreement with these emphatic words from serious academics. In November 1988, for example, the readership of the art magazine *art* learned that 'Even a layman would notice that the helmet sits "wrongly" on the head: something about the perspective appears to be not quite right. Experts found further shortcomings. Art historian Jan Kelch ... writes ... that the alternation of light and shade in the face would have to be more marked ...' The examinations with the atomic reactor led to the belittlement of that which was already known and had long been felt to be brilliant.

The Man with the Golden Helmet is not an isolated case. Famous paintings such as *David Playing the Harp before Saul* (ill. p. 192) and *The Polish Rider* (ill. p. 195) have also been devalued by the dismissive remark 'Studio of Rembrandt'. Since 1968 the Rembrandt Research Project, an extensive research project in the Netherlands, has been endeavouring to paint a clear picture of the artist's work and to separate the really authentic paintings from those for which Rembrandt's studio was responsible. 1989 saw the publication of the third volume of findings to date. Rembrandt's most famous work, *The Night Watch*, is the last picture with which it deals. It will thus be a few more years or even decades before research in this field is complete, until all of the works attributed to Rembrandt and signed 'Rembrandt' have been examined in detail and their authenticity checked by all available means. The Rembrandt Research Project is still dependent, however, on 'inadequate' X-rays, infra-red examinations and suchlike; an atomic reactor has not been made available.

The question arises as to whether the expense incurred in order to filter out the artist's work from that of those directly associated with him, without really being able to achieve results which are genuinely assured in the long run, is justified. In the first volume of *A Corpus of Rembrandt Paintings* the research team reattributed to pupils two portraits signed by Rembrandt in 1632 and housed in the Metropolitan Museum in New York. Shortly beforehand, however, American colleagues using a neutron activation autoradiograph had come to the conclusion that these pictures were indeed painted by Rembrandt himself. Despite the various articles written and the meetings which took place between the Dutch and American researchers, agreement could not be reached. Both paintings and a few others in American collections continue to be attributed to Rembrandt by the Americans whilst Dutch researchers dispute that he painted them.

Regardless of how competent the scientists may be, then, doubts exist as to whether particular paintings are really Rembrandt's own work. Given the amount being spent, one is forced to ask what is behind such endeavours in terms of interest in the findings. Is it important that we should know whether a picture was painted by Rembrandt or may only be labelled 'Rembrandtesque'? Is the cult of the genius which existed in the nineteenth century in particular blossoming anew? At the time it was responsible for many attributions which are now once again being seriously questioned. And when the authenticity of a painting is questioned, its value is lost. What was once regarded in Kassel as a genuine Rembrandt, the *Bearded Old Man with a Golden Chain* of 1632 (ill. p. 193), has been exposed by the Rembrandt Research Project 'as a painting "from a foreign hand" ... If the diagnosis is correct, then the very important Rembrandt collection ... has lost another gem.'[46] A judgement of this kind is based on concepts of the individuality of the artist the like of which did not exist in the seventeenth century and with which Rembrandt's methods are not compatible.

Rembrandt the entrepreneur was the head of a large studio practice, but it was always important to him that his style and compositional schemes were the only ones used. Pictures which he could not have painted himself either were not signed by him or did not leave his studio at all.

Outside the studio too there were several painters who seized upon Rembrandt's innovations and - by imitating Rembrandt - propagated his ideas. To this extent, all pictures which were painted at the same time and in Rembrandt's style were based on his ideas. In Rembrandt's opinion, it would therefore be perfectly logical to continue to regard them as masterpieces.

'Rembrandt'
*Bearded Old Man
with a Golden Chain,* 1632
Wood, 59.3 x 49.3 cm. Bredius 152
Kassel, Staatliche
Kunstsammlungen

'Rembrandt'
Joseph Accused by
Potiphar's Wife, 1655
Canvas, 106 x 98 cm. Bredius 523
Washington, National Gallery of
Art

In recent years the Rembrandt Research Project has come in for
increased criticism for a variety of reasons. For example, in the preface to
his monograph Gary Schwartz writes:

'The reader is no doubt aware that there is barely a drawing or painting in existence the attribution of which to Rembrandt has never been
questioned ... Whereas Rembrandt himself is considered as unique an
artist as ever lived, his individual works are so lacking in uniqueness that
they are constantly being assigned to other hands. ... In my view, it is of
much greater historical importance to know whether - and for whom -
Rembrandt painted or inspired the painting of a particular composition at
a particular moment in his career, than to know whether this or that
existing canvas is by the master's own hand.'[47]

In the introduction to her book, Svetlana Alpers, who was in fact the
first to use the term 'entrepreneur' in relation to Rembrandt, writes, 'What
we see before us is a growing number of pictures like *The Man with the
Golden Helmet* which - whether painted by him or not - would have been

'Rembrandt'
The Polish Rider, c. 1657
Canvas, 116.8 x 134.9 cm
Bredius 279
New York, The Frick Collection

unthinkable without Rembrandt. It is not the concept of human genius which merits attention, but the way in which it manifests itself.'[48] She concludes her work *Rembrandt als Unternehmer (Rembrandt as an Entrepreneur)* with the words:

'For the most part Rembrandt was himself responsible for the questions thrown up by the case of *The Man with the Golden Helmet.* ... It is no surprise to us that *The Man with the Golden Helmet* was regarded as a valid Rembrandt. Moreover, it retains its validity even if its authenticity is in question. The painting may not be his own work, but the old man remains a character from the house of Rembrandt - a painter whose undertakings cannot be reduced to *œuvres* from his own hand.'[49]

There is thus indeed justification for continuing to link with Rembrandt pictures which are not in fact his own work, for including them when we look at the development and interpretation of this artist and for continuing to treat them as works of outstanding importance in the collections to which they belong.

45 Cit. in Alpers 1989, p. 25

46 *art* 3/85, p. 54

47 Schwartz 1985, p. 11

48 Alpers 1989, p. 28

49 ibid., p. 264

Bibliography

This bibliography contains first the works quoted in the text and then the major works on Rembrandt which - without having been mentioned separately - were consulted in the preparation of this book. Given the wealth of literature available on the subject of Rembrandt, it cannot, of course, be anything approaching complete.

Literature quoted in the text

Alpers, Svetlana, *Rembrandt als Unternehmer. Sein Atelier und der Markt*, Cologne 1989
Copplestone, Trewin, *Rembrandt*, published by Hamlyn, London 1960
Goldscheider, Ludwig, *Rembrandt, Paintings, Drawings and Etchings*, London 1960
Haak, Bob, *Das Goldene Zeitalter der holländischen Malerei*, Cologne 1984
Hamann, Richard, *Rembrandts Radierungen*, Berlin [1]1905, [3]1920
Nash, J. M., *The Age of Rembrandt and Vermeer*, published by Phaidon, Oxford 1972
Rembrandt Research Project, *A Corpus of Rembrandt Paintings.* Edited by J. Bruyn, B. Haak, S. H. Levine, P. J. J. van Thiel, E. van de Wetering, The Hague/Boston/London, Vol. I 1982, Vol. II 1986, Vol. III 1989
Rosenberg, Jakob, *Rembrandt. Life and Work*, published by Phaidon, Oxford 1980
Schama, Simon, *Überfluß und schöner Schein*, Munich 1988
Schwartz, Gary, *Rembrandt - his life, his paintings*, London 1985
Tümpel, Christian, *Rembrandt. Mythos und Methode* (with contributions from Astrid Tümpel), Königstein in Tirol 1986

Further literature on Rembrandt

Bartsch, A., *Catalogue raisonné de tout les estampes qui forment l'œuvre de Rembrandt et ceux de ses principaux imitateurs*, Vol. 2, Vienna 1797
Bauch, K., *Der frühe Rembrandt und seine Zeit. Studien zur geschichtlichen Bedeutung seines Frühstils*, Berlin 1960
Bauch, K., *Rembrandt. Gemälde*, Berlin 1966
Benesch, O., *The Drawings of Rembrandt*, second edition, edited by Eva Benesch, 6 vols., London 1973
Bode, W. von, *Rembrandt und seine Zeitgenossen*, Leipzig 1906
Bredius, A., *Rembrandt. Gemälde*, Vienna 1935
Bredius-Gerson, A., *Rembrandt. The Complete Edition of the Paintings*, revised by H. Gerson, London 1969
Gerson, H., *Rembrandt. Paintings*, London 1968
Haak, B., *Rembrandt. Sein Leben, sein Werk, seine Zeit*, New York/Cologne 1969
Haak, B., *Rembrandt: Leben und Werk*, Cologne 1976

Hofstede de Groot, C., *Die Urkunden über Rembrandt (1575-1721)*, The Hague 1906

Langbehn, J., *Rembrandt als Erzieher*, Leipzig 1890

Münz, L., *Rembrandt*, Cologne 1967 (published in shortened form in London, 1984)

Neumann, C., *Rembrandt*, 2 vols., fourth edition, Munich 1924

Reiling, N. (Anna Seghers), *Jude und Judentum im Werke Rembrandts*, 1924, third edition, Leipzig 1990

Rosenberg, J., *Rembrandt*, 2 vols., second edition, London 1964 (quoted from the fourth edition, Oxford 1980)

Simson, O. von and J. Kelch, *Neue Beiträge zur Rembrandt-Forschung*, Berlin 1973

Strauss, W. and M. van der Meulen, *The Rembrandt Documents*, New York 1979

Sumowski, W., *Gemälde der Rembrandt-Schüler*, 5 vols., Landau/Pfalz 1983

Tümpel, C., *Rembrandt in Selbstzeugnissen und Bilddokumenten*, Reinbek near Hamburg 1977

Valentiner, W. R., *Rembrandt*, Stuttgart 1908

Vogel-Köhn, D., *Rembrandts Kinderzeichnungen*, Cologne 1981

Index

Adriaensdr., Alijdt 117

Alba, Duke of 10

Alpers, Svetlana 21, 39, 145, 148, 153, 159, 161, 194

Anslo, Cornelis Claesz. 54, 55

Arminius, Jacob 11

Backer, Jacob 115

Baldinucci, Filippo 18, 118

Bambeeck, Nicolaes van 118

Bas, Agatha 119

Benesch, Otto 21

Blankert, Albert 187

Braques, Georges 39

Bredius, Abraham 21

Brinkmann, P.H. 73

Bruyningh, Nicolaes 145

Burgundy, Mary of 8

Calkoen, Gysbert 53

Calvin, John 8, 11

Caravaggio 28, 30, 123

Castiglione, Baldassare 105

Charles V, emperor 8

Cocq, Frans Banning 115, 117, 118, 121

Cromwell, Oliver 92

Decker, Jeremias de 175, 177

Deyman, Johan 51, 53

Dircx, Geertghe 7, 123, 134, 161

Dou, Gerrit 6, 25

Dürer, Albrecht 79, 176

Dyck, Anthony van 176

Elison, Johannes 48, 55

Elsheimer, Adam 32

Eyck, Jan van 126

Flinck, Govert 107, 110, 112, 115, 120, 143, 182, 183

Fokkens, Melchior 183

Frederick V, prince-elector of the Palatinate, the Winter King, 63, 65

Frederik Hendrik, stadtholder 6, 10, 11, 39, 45, 63, 65, 67, 69, 79

Geer, Marguerite de 167

Gerson, Horst 21, 141

Gheyn, Jakob II de 122

Gheyn, Jakob III de (the Younger) 63, 68, 69

Gogh, Vincent van 102

Gomarus, Franciscus 11

Goudt, Hendrick 29, 32

Graeff, Wendela 159

Guercino 177

Haak, Bob 110

Hamann, Richard 147

Henry IV of France 63

Holbein the Younger, Hans 29

Honthorst, Gerrit van 65, 67, 68

Hoogstraeten, Samuel van 15, 30, 32, 118

Houbraken, Arnold 20, 107

Huygens, Christiaen 39

Huygens, Constantijn 6, 39, 40, 43, 45, 62, 65, 67, 68, 69, 71, 73, 134

Huygens, Maurits 62, 68

James I of England 63

Jans, Griet 49, 54

Jordaens, Jacob 176, 182

Josephus, Flavius 36, 79

Jouderville, Isaac 105

Keil, Bernhardt 118

Kelch, Jan 192

Laban, Ferdinand 191

Langbehn, Julius 20

Lastman, Pieter 6, 25, 26, 39, 50, 107, 137, 173

Leyden, Lucas van 176

Lievens, Jan 6, 25, 39, 40, 43, 44, 65, 67, 94, 182

Liotard, Jean-Etienne 137

Loo, Magdalena van 7, 167, 184

Lopez, Alfonso 103, 105

Luther, Martin 8

Mander, Karel van 15, 78, 79

Mantegna, Andrea 53

Margaret of Parma 9

Maurits of Nassau 10, 11, 63

Medici, Maria de 121
Menasseh ben Israel 89, 92
Michelangelo 40, 176

Oldenbarnevelt, Johan van 11, 28
Orlers, Jan 23, 25, 39, 40

Panofsky, Erwin 76, 77
Philip II of Spain 9, 10
Picasso, Pablo 39
Poussin, Nicolas 176

Raphael 40, 103, 105, 166, 176
Rembrandt Research Project 110,
121, 130, 133, 192, 193, 194
Ribera, José de 176
Rijksen, Jan 49, 54, 55
Rijn, Adriaen van 191
Rijn, Cornelia van (various daugh-
ters of Rembrandt) 6, 7, 56, 183
Rijn, Harmen Gerritsz. van 6, 22
Rijn, Rombertus van 6, 56
Rijn, Titia van 7, 184
Rijn, Titus van 7, 56, 117, 122, 123,
151, 152, 153, 154, 167, 183, 184
Rosenberg, Jacob 191
Rubens, Peter Paul 13, 65, 67, 69,
71
Ruffo, Don Antonio 176, 177, 178,
179, 180, 181, 183
Ruts, Nicolaes 52, 55
Ruytenburgh, Willem van 121

Sandrart, Joachim von 18, 105, 115
Schouten, Aeltje Gerritsdr. 54
Schrijver, Willem 159, 161
Schwartz, Gary 21, 26, 28, 76, 77,
134, 147, 159, 166, 167, 187, 194
Scriverius, Petrus 26, 28, 159
Seghers, Hercules Pietersz. 97, 100,
101
Six, Jan 142, 143, 145, 147
Solms, Amalia van 65, 67, 69
Soop, Floris 154
Stoffels, Hendrickje 7, 123, 152,
153, 154, 161, 183
Stuart, Elizabeth 63, 65
Suijtbroek, Cornelia (Neeltje) van
6, 22
Swanenburgh, Jakob Isaaksz. van
6, 22, 23
Sylvius, Johannes Cornelisz. 56

Titian 103, 176
Trip, Jacob 167
Trip, Maria 116
Tronchin, François 137
Tulp, Nicolaes 50, 51, 52, 53, 54,
122
Tümpel, Christian 21, 29, 32, 75,
130, 163, 166, 167, 173, 187

Uylenburgh, Aaltje 56
Uylenburgh, Hendrick 6, 48, 49,
50, 56, 153, 184
Uylenburgh, Rombertus 56
Uylenburgh, Saskia 6, 56, 59, 60,
62, 73, 75, 79, 95, 110, 117, 122, 123,
140, 143, 151, 161
Uylenburgh, Titia 122
Uyttenbogaert, Johannes 11, 55

Valerius, Adrianus 86
Vesalius, Andreas 51, 52, 53
Vos, Jan 143

Wagenaar, Jan 183
Weyden, Roger van der 126
William of Orange 9, 10, 56, 63

Photo credits

Archiv für Kunst und Geschichte,
Berlin
Joachim Blauel, Artothek,
Peissenberg
Blauel / Gnamm, Artothek,
Peissenberg
BPK, Berlin
A. Held, Ecublens
B.P. Keiser, Braunschweig
Rheinisches Bildarchiv, Cologne
RMN, Paris
Gerhard Reinhold, Leipzig-
Mölkay
and the photo libraries of the col-
lections mentioned in the captions.

The author and publisher wish to
thank the museums, galleries and
private collections for the permission to reproduce in this volume
paintings from their collections.